Women's Inspirational Daily Prayer

Following in the Footsteps of Female Saints and Holy Women

D1115407

Suzanne Haraburd

Women's Inspirational Daily Prayer—Following
in the Footsteps of Female Saints and Holy Women
©2012 by Suzanne Haraburd

First Edition

Printed in the United States of America

Haraburd Publishing, Ltd.
River Forest, Illinois 60305
sharaburd@sbcglobal.net

Cover art by Deco Bernadette Freeman

Library of Congress Control Number: 2012914432
ISBN: 13: 978-1478378457

1. Women   2. Prayer   3. Inspiration(al)   4. Daily   5. Saints
6. Holy   7. Scripture   8. Bible

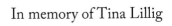

In memory of Tina Lillig

Table of Contents

Introduction

This book was born of my efforts to send a daily prayer to a friend who was being treated for breast cancer. I sought prayers and Bible portions that might uplift and strengthen her, and help her come closer to God. After sending a prayer a day for about 9 months, I could no longer easily find suitable prayers.

In many prayers, there was an emphasis on sin and the unworthiness of the supplicant that I feared might weaken rather than strengthen my friend. A woman already humbled by illness does not need to be preached to about humility; she needs to be raised up. A woman already suffering is not consoled by being told that suffering is a virtue. A woman already supporting her family physically, emotionally, and materially does not need to be told to be selfless. Yet these are the themes often found in devotional materials.

Most prayers refer to the supplicant as a man, and humanity as men. Most of the holy people held up as models are men. During my many years in the church as a catechist working almost entirely with women, and formed and supported by eminent, holy women, the constant references to men grated on me. There seems to be little recognition of women beyond devotion to Mary, the mother of God, and the qualities attributed to her make her seem far beyond the realities of women's daily life.

Where is the word that will speak to women? I heard it in the Catechesis of the Good Shepherd, an approach to religious formation for children ages 3 to 12, and their adult catechists. Over 50 years ago, Dr. Sofia Cavalletti, a Catholic Hebrew scholar, and her collaborator, Montessorian Gianna Gobbi, discovered that the child's way of going to God is different than that of the adult. Rather than the "royal Way of the Holy Cross" the child points out to us the "royal Way of Holy Joy." This path resembles that desired by Dietrich Bonhoeffer, who observed how often we turn to God only when our own resources fail. Bonhoeffer wished "to speak to God, not on the boundaries but at the center, not in weakness but in strength; and therefore not in death and guilt but in . . . life and goodness." [1]

The Catechesis nurtures our relationship with God, who desires our friendship love. Deep within each of us lies the heart of the 3-year-old child who waits, unknowingly, to hear God's words of love and who responds with her whole being. This is the reality I wanted to support in my friend. It is the reality I present here, the result of over 20 years of working with children in the Catechesis, years of prayer, thought, and study.

The dynamic in the kingdom of God is this: God invites and we respond. Christ, the Good Shepherd, constantly seeks us, his sheep, to live in loving relationship with him. When we respond to his call, we experience life to the full. Jesus said, "I have said these things to you so that my joy may be in you, and that your joy may be complete." (Jn 15:11) Joy in relationship with God is the goal of these prayers.

---

[1] Sofia Cavalletti, *Way of Holy Joy; Selected Writings of Sofia Cavalletti,* Patricia Coulter, transl. and ed. (Chicago, Liturgy Training Publications, 2011), p. 33.

How to use this book

This book was designed for women who are new to prayer, and for those who pray and want a resource to help them to go deeper. For those who have not yet developed the habit of daily prayer, I hope this book will entice you to do so. The scripture verses and prayers are short to make it easy for you to fit prayer into your life. The prayers are informative and provocative to give you food for thought and for your own prayers throughout the day. You will find footnotes attached to many of the prayers to make sources readily accessible to you.

Although the format of the book follows the calendar year, its themes are based on the liturgical year of the church, which begins with Advent, the four weeks of preparation leading up to Christmas; then Epiphany, the time after Christmas; then a few weeks of ordinary time followed by Lent, the time of preparation for Easter; then the season of Easter that ends with Pentecost, the feast of the Holy Spirit; finally, there are the long weeks of ordinary time at the end of the church year. The liturgical color for ordinary time is green. In the Catechesis, we call ordinary time growing time because that is the time when we use the gifts God has given us during the great feasts of Christmas, Easter, and Pentecost to grow in our relationship with God. Just as the church year is cyclical, so is this book, and you can begin it at any point in the year.

If you want to find a prayer that relates to a certain verse from the Bible, you will find an index of Bible citations in the back of the book to facilitate your search.

The Bible citations are mainly from the *Jerusalem Bible* and the *New Revised Standard Version;* a few are from *The New Greek English Interlinear New Testament* [2] or Everett Fox's translation of Torah, *The Five Books of Moses.*[3]

Finally, a word about the holy women honored in these pages. In 2010, the Episcopal church published a new book, *Holy Women, Holy Men,*[4] establishing feast days for both recognized saints and other women and men who proclaimed the gospel with their lives. The feast days for female saints and holy women are marked here with a quote either by or about them, followed by a Bible verse and a prayer. I hope you, like me, will be inspired by their example.

---

[2] Wheaton, IL, Tyndale House Publishers, 1990.
[3] New York, Schocken Books, 1995.
[4] *Holy Women, Holy Men; Celebrating the Saints* (New York, Church Publishing, 2010).

January:
the Season of Epiphany —
Following the Star

January 1

I see him, but not now; I behold him, but not near —
a star shall come out of Jacob,
and a scepter shall rise out of Israel.
Numbers 24:17

The year begins with mystery: a vision seen as if in a dream, beheld with longing deeper than memory for love dimly remembered yet unforgettable. This love beckons me as the star beckoned the magi, with a magnetic, visceral, irresistible attraction. Was this what Abraham felt when he heard, "Go you forth! Leave your land and your father's house and go to the place that I will show you."(Gen 12:1)? Where is the place that You will show me? Give me courage to follow the star.

January 2

*Does not wisdom call, and does not understanding
raise her voice?*
Proverbs 8:1

The magi, being wise, recognized and heeded the call of Wisdom. Wisdom calls me, too, but am I wise? Do I think that following the star is for religious people, artists, and other dreamers, but not for me? I'll be wise later, after I get some things done. After all, isn't the story of Christ's birth just that: a story, useful to tell children and provide atmosphere at Christmas time? Is there really a message there for me? Why am I reluctant to admit that I hope so? In my heart, I have long been aching for the One who loves me completely, just as I am. Could that One be You?

January 3

O send out your light and your truth; let them lead me;
let them bring me to your holy hill and
to your dwelling.
Psalm 43:3

*F*ollowing the star is an awesome quest, one like Maria's in *The Sound of Music,* that will take all the love I can give it, every day of my life. But how can I follow the star when I can't see the path ahead? Jesus answers, "I am the light of the world. Whoever follows me will never walk in darkness but will have the light of life." (Jn 8:12) I wonder who was luckier: the people who knew Jesus when He walked the earth, or those of us alive today? I can't see His earthly body or sense His physical presence. On the other hand, because Jesus died and rose again, His light and life are available to me wherever I am and whenever I need it. Thank You for being a lamp to my feet.

January 4 — Elizabeth Seton
Founder of the American Sisters of Charity

"The problem then of how to pray, and the problem of how to live — the two are the same problem — is the process of becoming ever more aware of the Holy Spirit within us. It is also a matter of learning to distinguish God's presence in the various life situations in which we find ourselves." [1]

"He goes ahead of them, and the sheep follow him because they know his voice."
John 10:4

Time after time, throughout salvation history, Your people find You on the mountain. Jesus went up the mountain to pray to You. There You helped him repulse Satan's temptation; there He was transfigured and revealed as the Messiah. I am most comfortable with my American, private faith, but Isaiah challenges me to move out of my comfort zone. This news is too wonderful to keep to myself. Where is the high place where I can announce Your presence? In Jesus' final appearance to the disciples, on a mountain, He told them, "Go, make disciples of all the nations, and know that I am with you always."(Mt 28:16-20) The high place is any place I can proclaim Your presence. Give me the courage today to share the good news with someone.

---

[1] Vermaelen, Elizabeth S.C. (1997) "Decision Making in the Life of Elizabeth Ann Seton," *Vincentian Heritage Journal:* Vol. 18: Iss. 2, Article 6, p. 216. Available at: http://via.library,depaul.edu/vhj/vol18/iss2/6

January 5

※

Arise, shine out, for your light has come, the glory of the Lord is rising on you, though night still covers the earth and darkness the peoples.
Isaiah 60:1

*E*ven in darkness the prophet Isaiah sees the star. As I walk, preoccupied with worries, he calls: arise! What does he see that I don't see? Not with the eyes of his body but with the eyes of faith, he sees Your glory, like a tiny beam of light in the night sky soon to blaze more brightly than the sun. Isaiah also sees me, like a moon in the early morning sky, shining in Your reflected light. Thank You for sending Your messengers, the prophets, to hearten me and remind me to walk, head up, in Your light.

January 6 — Epiphany

They set out; and there, ahead of them, went the star
that they had seen at its rising, until it stopped over the place
where the child was. The sight of the star
filled them with delight.
Matthew 2:9-10

So this is it. This is what the journey is all about, what Your deepest desire is for me. Just this: to recognize You in the child; to be stunned into speechless delight; to fall on my knees in grateful wonder and praise, filled with unimaginable joy. On this day, let me not be in a hurry to leave. Let me rest here, to enjoy and celebrate the marvelous gift that is born in my heart.

January 7

How you are fallen from heaven,
O Day Star, son of Dawn!
Isaiah 14:12

*W*ho is this child? The question is impossible to answer; nevertheless, like me, the Jews of long ago needed a word of hope, and so Isaiah tries to describe the indescribable: Day Star, son of Dawn, Wonderful Counselor, Mighty God, Everlasting Father, Prince of Peace, Immanuel: God-with-us. These majestic, heroic names could only hint at the astonishing reality: that the long-anticipated messiah came in the form of a small baby born to a family undistinguished except in its lineage, accompanied by more than a whiff of scandal. Who is this child? Give me the grace to not think I know the answer, for You are so much greater than I can imagine.

January 8 — Harriet Bedell, Deaconess and Missionary

🪺

An Episcopal missionary among the Cheyenne Indians in Oklahoma, Bedell cared for the sick and the poor, organized social services for the tribe, performed the duties of the rector in his absence, and provided education for the women and children. She later organized a boarding school in a remote area of Alaska. Finally, she lived with the Seminole Indians in Florida and worked with them to improve their quality of life.[2]

"Whoever serves me must follow me, and where I am, there will my servant be also."
John 12:26

*W*ho are You, Jesus, and how came You to me? Like Mary on hearing the angel's words, after the first dazzle is over, I, too, am disturbed. I didn't know how dark my life was until You broke in like dawn, shining light on things I thought I had put behind me. Following the star has not, after all, taken me *away* from people and things that I don't want to think about; rather, it is a journey *through* or *with* them. On the way You restore my soul. You lead me through the gloomy valley. You set a luxurious table before me. (Ps 23) When I become discouraged on the journey, let me remember that Jesus came so that I might have life to the full. (Jn 10:10)

---

[2] http://www.floridamemory.com/photographiccollection/collections/?id=2

January 9 — Julia Chester Emery, Missionary

She went forth "with hope for enlargement of vision, opening up new occasions for service, acceptance of new tasks." [3]

Then Jesus told his disciples, "If any want to become my followers, let them deny themselves and take up their cross and follow me."
Matthew 16:24

*M*y call was not to mission work; nevertheless, like Julia Chester Emery, I went forth. I left my previous life and put aside other goals in order to become a mother, a sacrifice I made joyfully in return for the priceless gift of children. Like every mother, I have carried my cross, yet Emery's words help me realize that motherhood brought me gifts beyond the joys and sorrows of daily life. Motherhood enlarged my vision, gave me new occasions for service, and new tasks through which to serve You. Thank You for allowing me to tread the path of motherhood as I follow the star.

---

[3] *Holy Women, Holy Men;* p. 162.

January 10

Going into the house they saw the child with his
mother Mary, and falling to their knees they did him homage.
Matthew 2:11

*W*hen have I ever fallen to my knees in joy and awe, either literally or metaphorically? I'm a little to cool for that, a little too skeptical. I like to keep my reactions to myself, to question the gift. Is it really that great? If I open my heart wide enough to fully receive the gift of Your love will I still be me? I feel safer standing at a distance with my familiar pain. Is this what happened to Adam and Eve when they ate the fruit of the tree of the knowledge of good and evil? Did they suddenly understand Who You are and the enormity of Your love? Did it scare them so much that they tried to hide from You? Lord, forgive my fear and reluctance. Give me the courage not to hide, but to walk with You in Your garden of love.

January 11

Those who seek me eagerly shall find me.
Proverbs 8:17

I seek something eagerly when I anticipate joy at finding it. The anticipation of joy usually comes from a previous experience. "It was you who created my inmost self, and put me together in my mother's womb." (Ps 139:13) You are deep in my heart's memory. There is not a time when I did not know Your love; I couldn't leave You if I tried; and yet, I get distracted. My attention wanders far from You. I am unhappy and I wonder why. May each night sky remind me who loved me first and best, whose love is unfailing: the One whose star I am following.

January 12

*Then, opening their treasures, they offered him gifts of
gold and frankincense and myrrh.*
Matthew 2:11

*A*t the first Epiphany the magi fell to their knees, did Jesus
homage, then opened and offered their treasures to Him. My
epiphany was not a dramatic moment, but a slowly dawning
realization that put a sparkle in my eye, lightened my heart,
and tugged me gently yet relentlessly forward toward the
Light, toward You. I couldn't help myself, and I didn't want
to -- I couldn't -- deny what was happening, even during very
sad and difficult times. Jesus says, "For where your treasure is,
there your heart will be also." (Mt 6:21) In that moment of
epiphany, I gave mine to You.

January 13

Can we find anyone else like this — one in whom
is the spirit of God?
Genesis 41:38

*W*ho is this child? Throughout history, heroic people
have died for the sake of others: the Christian martyrs,
Ghandi, and Martin Luther King come to mind. Only one
person has risen again. Jesus alone bridges the otherwise-
insurmountable gap between heaven and earth, between You
and me. Through Christ, the gate, I enter Your kingdom;
in Christ I am mingled and disappear, like the water in the
wine; with Christ I offer myself to You in the bread and
the wine. This Christ is the One on whom I reflect in awe,
wonder and gratitude, as I follow the star.

January 14

But they were warned in a dream not to go back to
Herod, and returned to their own country by a different way.
Matthew 2:12

*H*aving found the child Jesus, the magi went home by a different way. When I began to realize that Jesus found me, my route home was utterly changed. "See, I am making all things new." (Rev. 21:5) Home is where You are, within me. (Jn 14:20) Like Abraham, I carry my home wherever I go, and wherever I go becomes a sacred place because You are with me. "The place that I will show you . . ." (Gen 12:1), the essential place without which nowhere can be home, is here, within me, the place where You are pleased to dwell.

January 15

🜨

*"Go from your country and your kindred and your father's
house to the land that I will show you.*
Genesis 12:1

*I*f You are everywhere why did Abraham have to leave home
and family to follow You? You said to him, "Go!" and Abraham
went, becoming a model of faith for every generation after
him. Jesus says, "Follow me," adding to the list of things
to leave behind: livelihood, money, and possessions. When
someone said to Jesus that His mother, brothers, and sisters
were waiting for Him, He said, "Who are my mother and
my brothers? Anyone who does the will of God, that person
is my brother and sister and mother." (Mk 3:32-35) These
are hard teachings. Help me know what to take with me and
what to leave behind as I follow the star.

January 16

*By paths they have not known I will guide them. I will turn
the darkness before them into light, the rough places
into level ground. These are the things I will do,
and I will not forsake them.*
Isaiah 42:16

Following the star, I am, like Abraham and the magi, on a
path not known to me. Only in darkness can I see the star.
Only in unknown territory do I seek a guide. Only on rough
ground do I reach for support. Did You send me on this
adventure so that I would know this place, the place where
You dwell, for the first time?

> We shall not cease from exploration
> And the end of all our exploring
> Will be to arrive where we started
> And know the place for the first time. [4]

---

[4] T.S. Eliot, "Little Gidding" from his poem, "The Four Quartets."

January 17

*The Lord went in front of them in a pillar of cloud by day,
to lead them along the way, and in a pillar of fire by night,
to give them light, so that they might travel
by day and by night.*
Exodus 13:21

*A*s I follow the star, it's heartening to remember that I go no place where You are not. In darkness and in light you lead me, faithful to Your promises of old. At Jesus' baptism You spoke from the cloud, "This is my Son, the Beloved; listen to him!" (Mk 9:7) On the day of Pentecost, when tongues of fire came to rest on the heads of those assembled there, You sent Your Spirit to lead them, and me, to complete truth. (Acts 2:1-4, Jn 16:13) May I see You before me always.

January 18

*Trust in the Lord with all your heart, and do not
rely on your own insight. In all your ways acknowledge
him, and he will make straight your paths.*
Proverbs 3:5-6

*H*ow easily I fall into the trap of thinking I am alone on
this journey! It is a familiar habit. I try to figure everything
out in my mind before I make a move, and when I have a
problem, then -- and only then -- do I remember to pray to
You. Like a teenager, I would rather trust myself and cling to
the illusion that I can control the outcome. Soon I am on my
knees again begging You to get me out of yet another jam.
Today I will try it Your way. Following the advice of those
who trod this path before me, I will begin by trusting You,
not half- but whole-heartedly, praying for Your guidance
before I continue on my journey, following the star.

January 19

"Know that I am with you and will keep you wherever
you go, and will not leave you until I have done
what I have promised you."
Genesis 28:15

*W*ho is this child? One who is steadfast and faithful, who keeps the promises You made to the ancestors of long ago. When you appeared to Jacob in a dream, You promised never to abandon him, to stay with him and protect him wherever he went until You did all You promised. You made this promise not only to Jacob, but to all his descendants. Today Jesus reassures me with the same vow: "Know that I am with you always; yes, to the end of time." (Mt. 28:20) May I, like Jacob, awaken from my dream of self-sufficiency to exclaim, "Truly, God is in this place and I never knew it!"

January 20

So we have the prophetic message more fully confirmed.
You will do well to be attentive to this as to a lamp
shining in a dark place, until the day dawns and
the morning star rises in your hearts.
2 Peter 1:19

*N*ow I think I understand: the star is Jesus, the Morning Star (Rev 22:16), and the journey is one of the heart. I need go nowhere, but only close my eyes and be attentive to explore what Teresa of Avila calls my interior castle,[5] the place within my heart where You dwell. Teresa writes, "It is most important to withdraw from all unnecessary cares and business, as far as compatible with the duties of one's state of life." Somehow, it seems more acceptable to travel far and wide in search of You than to be still here and now. Give me the courage to take time to follow the star within my heart.

---

[5]http://www.sacred-texts.com/chr/tic/index.htm

January 21—St. Agnes, Martyr

✲

*St. Agnes is one of seven women, aside from the Blessed
Virgin Mary, commemorated by name in the Canon of the
Mass. Tradition teaches that Agnes, the daughter of a Roman
nobleman, suffered martyrdom at about age 12 after refusing to
marry the son of a Roman prefect.*[6]

*To everyone who conquers and continues to do my works
to the end, I will give authority, even as I also received
authority from my Father. To the one who conquers
I will also give the morning star.*
Revelation 2:26, 28-29

*A*gnes was 12 or 13 years old when she was condemned
to death for refusing to marry the son of a Roman official.
How can one so powerless be said to conquer anything?
When Jesus was silent before Pilate, Pilate asked Him, "Are
you refusing to speak to me? Surely you know I have power
to release you and I have power to crucify you?" (Jn 19:10)
Who had more power, Jesus or Pilate? Jesus did many deeds
of power on earth, including His death and -- the greatest
deed of all -- His resurrection. What kind of power did
Jesus have? The same power with which Agnes conquered
the Roman ruler who tried to exert his authority over her.
That, and not the power of this world, propels me toward
the star.

---

[6] http://en.wikipedia.org/wiki/Agnes_of_Rome

January 22

The angel said to him, "Fasten your belt and put on your
sandals." He did so. Then he said to him,
"Wrap your cloak around you and follow me."
Acts 12:8

*F*ollowing the star can be a wild ride. One moment I'm
cruising happily along with the wind in my hair, then, white-
knuckled, I'm careening out of control, my heart pounding
and adrenaline rushing through my veins. I imagine Jesus
sitting next to me calmly in the passenger seat. Like the
disciples in the storm with Jesus asleep in the boat, I want to
yell, "Master, we're going down!" Jesus says, "Take heart, it is
I; do not be afraid." (Mt 14:27) Again my ego has deceived
me. When I become fainthearted on the journey, help me
remember it's You, not me, in the driver's seat.

January 23

*Thus says the Lord: Stand at the crossroads, and look, and ask
for the ancient paths, where the good way lies;
and walk in it, and find rest for your souls.*
Jeremiah 6:16

*F*ollowing the star, I anticipate struggle, not rest. But Jesus
says, "Take my yoke upon you, and learn from me; for I am
gentle and humble in heart, and you will find rest for your
souls." (Mt 11:29) I hardly gave a thought to my soul before
I began to follow the star. On the journey, the light of Your
love illuminated the dark places in my soul. I discovered
how much I need the rest only You can provide. When I
struggle to take time to be alone with You, give me the grace
to remember that rest for my soul is the one thing necessary
to doing my best in any other endeavor.

January 24 — Ordination of Florence Li Tim-Oi, first woman priest in the Anglican Communion

Tim-Oi was a deacon in charge of an Anglican congregation thronged with Chinese refugees during the Second World War. When a priest could no longer travel from Japanese-occupied territory to preside at eucharist, she presided as a deacon. In 1944, the bishop of Hong Kong met her in Free China and ordained her a priest.[7]

Those who are wise shall shine like the brightness of the sky, and those who lead many to righteousness, like the stars forever and ever.
Daniel 12:3

*A*s I follow the star, other lights assist me: women and men of great courage and faith whose righteousness shines like a beacon on my path. Thirty years before the ordination of women was accepted in the Anglican Communion, Florence was ordained a priest during WWII, in response to the crisis among Anglican Christians in China caused by the Japanese invasion. What tremendous courage it must have taken to become a leader at such a dangerous time, knowing that as a woman, not only was she particularly vulnerable, but that many would reject her as a priest. When I face obstacles on my journey, may Florence's example inspire and strengthen me.

---

[7] *http://www.litim-oi.org/litim-oi.html*

January 25

In him was life, and the life was the light of all people.
The light shines in the darkness, and the darkness
did not overcome it.
John 1:4-5

*I*t is tempting to feel overwhelmed by the presence of evil. Evil is a reality upon which the news, television, and movies seem to love to dwell. The more connected I am to others, the more I am aware of suffering and death. Sometimes I want to escape into myself and hide from the world. On the other hand, You created us to live with You in community. Jesus' death and resurrection made us one with You as members of His Body. When I focus on evil instead of Christ I cut myself off from His Light, and injure His Body. Help me to remain faithful to You by keeping my eyes on Your Light, my star in the darkness.

January 26

Jacob said, "May it please my lord to go on ahead of his servant. For my part, I will move at a slower pace, to suit the flock I am driving and the children."
Genesis 33:14

Years after I quit my job to stay home with my daughter, I noticed that some of my peers, with children as well as careers, had traveled ahead of me. Fighting the temptation to envy, I thought about what I had done with my time. Mostly, I waited: for my toddler daughter to make her way down the sidewalk, stopping to investigate every dirty cigarette butt; for her to help me clean instead of doing it quickly by myself; for her ballet class to end; for her to read a book to me. I learned that my achievements don't define me. I learned to slow down, if not to relax, and to savor the small moments in life. Thank You for teaching me to move at the pace of the children as I follow the star.

January 27 — Sts. Lydia, Dorcas (Tabitha), and Phoebe, Witnesses to the Faith

I commend to you our sister Phoebe, a deaconess of the church at Cenchreae. Give her, in union with the Lord, a welcome worthy of saints, and help her with anything she needs: she has looked after a great many people, myself included.
Romans 16:1-2

When Jesus walked the earth, many women followed and provided for Him. (Mt 27:55) After His death and resurrection, the Bible tells of women, including Lydia, Dorcas, and Phoebe, who continued to work for Jesus' mission. Today women do Christ's work in much the same manner as the women of the New Testament: behind the scenes and often unacknowledged. I imagine that Lydia, Dorcas, and Phoebe don't care how they are remembered, but I want to give each one of them my heartfelt thanks for passing on the faith so that I can follow the star.

January 28

"I know them, and they follow me."
John 10:27

*H*ere is a miracle: You know me, and You still love me. For years I tried hard to figure out what others wanted and to provide it, hoping to get in return what passed for love. One day I heard, as if for the first time, that You know me and love me, just as I am. My joy at being known and loved by You gave me the courage I needed to stop trying for counterfeit love, and instead to do the things that bring me closer to You. What wondrous love is this that You should know me? I follow the star, buoyed by Your love for me.

January 29

Reveal the path of life to me, and give me unbounded
joy in your presence.
Psalm 16:8, 11

*T*his seems like a contradiction: a path is, by definition, bounded. Following a path, one is not free to wander just anywhere, one follows a particular route. Yet Your path of life, like a trick of physics, leads to a destination without bounds: not mere happiness, but joy unlimited by time, place, or circumstance; the kingdom of heaven in kairos time, the appointed time for Your purposes, absolutely free from the limits of this world. [8] On that path, the horizontal line of my life intersects with the vertical line of eternity, forming the cross which Jesus says I must carry in order to follow Him. Lead me on the royal road to joy!

---

[8] http://en.wikipedia.org/wiki/Kairos#In_Christian_theology

January 30

"I am the gate. Whoever enters by me will be saved, and will come in and go out and find pasture."
John 10:9

*H*ere is another seeming contradiction: a gate is a boundary, barring my way, yet those who enter by Jesus, the gate, find unlimited freedom to come and go. Having entered the sheepfold through Christ, my Shepherd, I know my home is eternally in You. Fear may overtake me, distractions may beckon, but Jesus the gate opens the way again. Now I know: "neither death, nor life, nor angels, nor rulers, nor things present, nor things to come, nor powers, nor height, nor depth, nor anything else in all creation, will be able to separate" me from You. (Rom. 8:38-39) Whether I come or go, nothing can bar my way as I follow the star.

January 31

✛

"It is I, Jesus, who sent my angel to you with this
testimony . . . . I am the root and the descendant of David,
the bright morning star."
Revelation 22:16

What has been prophesied, what has been written, what has been told: all this that I have, tremblingly, dared to hope for, burns brightly where, before, all seemed hopelessly dark. As I near the end of this month following the star, the pale light of dawn gives way to illumination. The truth has set me free on my journey, joyful in the knowledge that I am not alone and never have been. My restless search is over; the Star is within me, and I am in Him. As I travel, I sing a song of joy:

> Bright morning star a-rising,
> Bright morning star a-rising,
> Bright morning star a-rising,
> Day is a-breaking in my soul. [9]

---

[9]http://www.informatik.uni-hamburg.de/~zierke/peter.bellamy/songs/
brightmorningstar.html

February:
Winter Retreat

February 1—St. Brigid of Kildare

Saint Brigid was not given to sleep,
Nor was she intermittent about God's love of her. [1]

God, you examine me and know me.
Psalm 139:1

*I*n the cold, grey days of February I don't expect much
enjoyment, only to put each day behind me, one by one, as
I look forward to spring. But there has been a change; now
I know that You dwell within my heart. I am eager to learn
more about this mystery and about Your love for me. The
psalmist has also wondered. Psalm 139 is a kind of map, a
report of his discoveries, one that I will use as I embark upon
my own inner exploration. For once, I am grateful for the
bleak February weather. It creates a climate conducive to
going within.

---

[1] http://en.wikipedia.org/wiki/St._Brigid

February 2

You know if I am standing or sitting.
Psalm 139:2(a)

Standing, I wait, shop, cook, fold laundry, pray in church. Sitting, I watch, work, eat, drive, pray at home. None of this seems particularly interesting, even to me, and it is certainly nothing You haven't seen a few billion times before. Why do these small things matter to You? I have no position of power over people. Or do I? Maybe not power over but I do have power to "do justice, and to love kindness, and to walk humbly with" You. (Mic 6:8) Today I will speak the truth gently but firmly and make a helpful gesture, remembering with humility and joy that You are with me in all the activities of my life.

February 3

You read my thoughts from far away.
Psalm 139:2(b)

I'm just getting used to the idea that You are within me; now the psalmist says You are far away. What am I to think? Maybe I am the one who, like the prodigal son, has travelled far away from You, taking and unthinkingly spending Your gifts, until, in poverty and need, I turn back to You. "While he was still a long way off, his father saw him and was moved with pity." (Lk 15:20) Focused only on myself, I thought I was coming home to You, but no; You didn't stand still and wait; You ran to me. Clasped in your warm embrace, dumb with amazed joy, choking back tears, I finally get it: when You seem far away, it is I who need to return.

February 4

Whether I walk or lie down, you are watching.
Psalm 139:3(a)

You sent Your commandments, Your words, like guardian angels, to watch over me night and day. "When you walk, they will lead you; when you lie down, they will watch over you." (Prov 6:22) You sent Jesus, Your Word, to go ahead of me and lead me in right paths. He accompanies me through the gloomy valley and finds me when I run away. He makes me lie down in green pastures. (Ps 23:2-4) Today, as I walk, lie down, drive, sit, or stand, may I rest in the joyous knowledge that Your goodness and mercy are my constant companions.

February 5—Anne Hutchinson, Prophetic Witness

How did Abraham know that it was God that bid him offer his son, being a breach of the sixth commandment? . . . So to me by an immediate revelation . . . . By the voice of his own spirit to my soul. [2]

The word is not even on my tongue before you know all about it.
Psalm 139:4

Before a word comes out of my mouth, before I have even thought what to say, You know it; You listen that carefully to me. Do I listen to You? A prophet is one who, like Anne Hutchinson, listens to You with her whole soul and has the courage to tell people what she heard, regardless of the consequences. I like to think that I can play it safe, choosing what to say and what not to say. What if I realized that I am not alone in my thoughts? What if I listened to You as I do to a friend, instead of ignoring You as if You were a distant being? Teach me to rely on You. Help me learn to be quiet and listen for Your voice.

---

[2] http://www.constitution.org/primarysources/hutchinson.html

February 6

Close behind and close in front you fence me around,
shielding me with your hand.
Psalm 139:5

*W*hen my children were very small, more than anything they loved to move and explore, first scooting on their bellies, then crawling, then walking. Not wanting to discourage their zeal for exploration, I followed them around, using my body more than words to redirect them away from harm. These memories come to mind when I think of You shielding me with Your hand: an intimate, affectionate, tolerant, and patient protection. The fence, of course, is the sheepfold, my home. With Jesus, the gate and shepherd, I toddle happily in and out, safe within the hollow of Your hand. (Jn 10)

February 7

🎗

Such knowledge is beyond my understanding,
a height to which my mind
cannot attain.

Psalm 139:6

Like the people in Genesis who tried to build a tower to heaven, Adam and Eve thought they could attain the height of Your knowledge, and in the attempt, fell farther away from You. The psalmist is wiser. Secure in Your love, he is content to be Your child, and to let You be God. Sometimes I worry: am I smart enough? Accomplished enough? Paul teaches that in Your kingdom the most important accomplishment is not knowledge: "If I understand all mysteries and all knowledge, but do not have love, I am nothing." (1 Cor 13:2) All accomplishments are passing; only love never ends. If I am to attain to anything, let it be to love.

February 8

Where could I go to escape your spirit?
Where could I flee from your presence?
Psalm 139:7

*A*dam and Eve tried to flee from You. So did Jonah. Their efforts seem almost laughable. In my superior wisdom I chuckle, reminded of little children playfully trying to hide or run away, but these people were not playing; they were terrified. The psalmist is not afraid of You. Maybe he knows something that Adam, Eve, and Jonah did not know, something about who You are. Adam and Eve walked with you in the cool of the day, but in their ignorance and fear thought they could hide from You. Jonah heard Your voice, and in his ignorance and fear, he thought he could flee from You. And what about me? What makes me think that I am ever not in Your presence? Why do I ever believe that You are far away?

February 9

If I climb the heavens, you are there,
Psalm 139:8(a)

Jacob dreamed of a ladder reaching from earth to heaven, but he didn't have to climb the ladder to find You; You came down to him. (Gen 28:12-13) When Jesus was baptized, the heavens opened and You descended, alighting on Him like a dove. (Mt.3:16) Today, although a plane can take me from earth to the heavens, I don't need to go there to find You. In Jesus You came down to establish forever the ladder between heaven and earth. In Jesus, I am united with You right where I am, no matter where I am.

February 10

there too, if I lie in Sheol.
Psalm 139:8(b)

Growing up in the church, I was taught that if I did certain things, I would go to hell. When I was an adult, I knew someone who did one of those things, and I also knew that his life had been hell on earth. The psalmist says that if he is in hell, You are there with him, as You were with him in his hell on earth. But You did not merely remain with him in his torment; You sent Your Son, the Good Shepherd, to find and free him. "Christ died for the guilty to lead us to God." (1 Pet 3:18) After He died, He descended into hell to free all those held captive there by evil. Through His resurrection, "all beings, in the heavens, on earth and in the underworld" are united. (Phil 2:10) There is nowhere my Shepherd will not go to find his sheep.

February 11 — Frances Jane (Fanny) Van Alstyne Crosby, hymnwriter

※

Blessed assurance, Jesus is mine! O what a foretaste of glory divine!
Heir of salvation, purchase of God, born of His Spirit, washed in His blood. [3]

Let us approach God with a true heart in full assurance of faith.
Hebrews 10:22

𝓕anny Crosby was blind from birth, yet she became "the premier hymnist of the gospel song period," writing over 8,000 hymns, many, like "Blessed Assurance," still well-loved today.[4] When Jesus and the disciples encountered the man born blind, they asked Jesus whose fault, the man's or his parents', caused his blindness. Jesus said, "Neither this man nor his parents sinned; he was born blind so that God's works might be revealed in him." (Jn 9:2-3) I have sight, and yet, in the ways that matter to You, I am sometimes blind. "Mortals look at appearances but the Lord looks at the heart." (1 Sam 16:7) Heal my blindness; help me see the hearts of others so that Your works may be revealed in me!

---

[3] "Blessed Assurance," by Fanny Crosby, see http://www.hymntime.com/tch/htm/b/l/e/blesseda.htm
[4] ibid.

February 12

If I flew to the point of sunrise, or westward
across the sea, your hand would
still be guiding me,
Psalm 139:9-10

Jonah tried to flee from You by sailing to the ends of the earth, but when You unleashed a storm and violent wind on the sea he realized that he could not flee Your guiding hand. You put him in danger in order to save his life, and through him, the lives of the people of Ninevah. (Jon:1-2) After Jesus fed the five thousand, His disciples began to row a boat across the sea without Him. In the darkness, through a strong wind, they saw Jesus walking toward them on the rough sea, guiding the boat safely to shore. (Jn 6:12-21) In their danger, You guided them to new life so that they could help You to save countless people, including me. In the storms of life, help me remember that out of danger You bring new life, and the opportunity to help You save others.

February 13

your right hand holding me.
Psalm 139:10

*E*ven as I flee, You are holding me; only my ego deludes me into thinking I can elude You. Jesus said, "If any one of you here had only one sheep and it fell down a hole, would he not get hold of it and lift it out? How much more valuable is a human being than a sheep!" (Mt 12:11-12) A sheep may wander away, but the Good Shepherd will pursue that sheep until He finds it. (Jn 17:12) No matter how hard I try to run away, I can never outrun Your loving care for me.

February 14

If I asked darkness to cover me, and light to
become night around me, that darkness would not be dark to
you, night would be as light as day.
Psalm 139:11-12

There is more than one way to flee. Psychological distance, more than physical distance, is, like the darkness that fell over the land of Egypt, "a darkness that can be felt," (Ex 10:21) in which I feel helpless and utterly alone. Yet the psalmist says that You are there in the full light of day. In Jesus, Your command, "Let there be light!" is realized in a total way. On the day of His death, darkness covered the land *until* the moment of His death; at the very moment that darkness seemed to win, the Light triumphed once and for all.
(Mt 27:45) Jesus says, "I have come as light into the world, so that everyone who believes in me should not remain in the darkness." (Jn 12:46) May I always remember that in the darkness of the tomb You brought an entirely new kind of light into the world, a light unlimited by time, space -- and my perceptions.

February 15

It was you who created my inmost self,
Psalm 139:13(a)

*W*hat does it mean that You created my inmost self? That there is something miraculous inside of me, something of You. What could that miraculous something be? In the Book of Exodus, You told Moses to make you a shrine so that You could dwell in Your people. (Ex 25:8) That shrine is within me, too. The Holy of Holies, Your dwelling place, is in my heart. My body is the temple of Your Holy Spirit. (1 Cor 6:19) I am not my own; You created me so that You could dwell within me. May I live each day remembering that.

February 16

and put me together in my mother's womb;
Psalm 139:13(b)

*Y*ou made a covenant with Abraham, promising to make him the father of many nations. (Gen 17) Abraham fulfilled his promise by circumcising himself and all his men, while You fulfilled your promise in the womb of Sara and her female descendants. When Mary visited her pregnant cousin, Elizabeth, to share the news of Jesus' coming, Elizabeth saw within Mary's womb the long-awaited Messiah and exclaimed, "Blessed is the fruit of your womb!" (Lk 1:42) Could it be that Your greatest work is performed, not in the vastness of creation, but in a place absolutely hidden from view? I, too, have been created by You within my mother's womb. What part of Your divine plan is unfolding within me?

February 17

for all these mysteries I thank you: for the wonder of myself,
for the wonder of your works.
Psalm 139:14

A mystery, like love, is something that is difficult or impossible to understand or explain. Like love, Your mysteries fill me with joyous, bewildered wonder. Elated, I walk on air, fairly bursting with joy, wanting to tell the whole world : You who are love, love me! My heart swells with a song of praise:

> O Lord my God! When I in awesome wonder
> Consider all the worlds Thy hands have made.
> I see the stars, I hear the rolling thunder,
> Thy power throughout the universe displayed.
>
> Then sings my soul, my Saviour God, to Thee;
> How great Thou art, how great Thou art!
> Then sings my soul, my Saviour God, to Thee:
> How great Thou art, how great Thou art! [5]

---

[5] http://en.wikipedia.org/wiki/How_Great_Thou_Art_%28hymn%29

February 18

You know me through and through,
from having watched my bones take shape when I was being
formed in secret, knitted together in the
limbo of the womb.
Psalm 139:15

*I*n secret, You wait and watch for Your purposes to be accomplished. Buried in the earth, hidden seeds are transformed and given new life; in the darkness of the womb, invisible cells are transformed and a child is formed. You give me these "treasures of darkness and riches hidden in secret places" so that I may know that it is You who calls me by name. (Is 45:3) What is the name by which, in calling, You create me? I will close my eyes and be silent now so that in secret, in the darkness, I may hear my name and know myself as You do.

February 19

You had scrutinized my every action, all were
recorded in your book, my days listed and determined,
even before the first of them occurred.
Psalm 139:16-17

*H*ow do I reconcile this with a lifetime of being told that I had to be very careful what choices I make in life? You set before me the choice of life or death, blessing or curse, and said I must choose. (Deut 30:19) Your Son told me what I need to do to follow Him and enter into Your kingdom. Yet the psalmist says that You have long known what my choices will be. What is the message hidden within this paradox? As I contemplate this and other paradoxes of my life with You, may I not miss the fundamental message of Your loving care for me.

February 20

God, how hard it is to grasp your thoughts!
How impossible to count them!
Psalm 139:17

I know that Your thoughts are not my thoughts, nor Your ways my ways (Is 55:8), but that doesn't stop me from having a lot of questions. Dare I ask them? Who are You? What are You like? Why do I matter to You? Why do you let me make bad choices? Why do disasters happen to innocent people? Like Eve, I wish to eat the fruit of the Tree of the Knowledge of Good and Evil. When, upon hearing that Jesus had to die, the disciples asked why, Jesus put a small child next to Himself, saying, "Whoever welcomes this child in my name welcomes me, and whoever welcomes me welcomes the one who sent me." (Lk 9:47) When I get distracted with the "why" question, bring my attention back to welcoming You in the child.

February 21

I could no more count them than I could the sand,
and suppose I could, you will still be with me.
Psalm 139:18

*L*ike me, the psalmist engages in magical thinking. I want so badly to feel like I have a grip on reality. I obsess about You as if I believe that, by thinking about You long enough, I might comprehend the totality of Your thoughts, and establish my independence of You. Like an autistic person who counts days, weeks, and years, or a man who counts his money, or a small boy who counts his baseball cards, I seek order to control my existence. The psalmist points out my delusion. Even if I could count Your thoughts, I could never distance You from me.

February 22

God, if only you would kill the wicked! Men of blood,
away from me! They talk blasphemously about you,
regard your thoughts as nothing.
Psalm 139:19-20

*L*istening to the news, reading the paper, hearing about innocent people being traumatized and killed by the wicked, I get angry. What kind of God lets them get away with their crimes? I can imagine what the oppressed Jewish people felt, hearing Jesus, one of their own, tell them that You are kind to the wicked. (Lk 6:35) Even Paul had no kind word for the wicked. Wouldn't our world be better without them? Wouldn't Your kingdom finally come? On the other hand, Jesus also said, "Let anyone among you who is without sin be the first to throw a stone." (Jn 8:7) Thank you for Your loving kindness and the gift of Your mercy, from which I benefit more than I know.

February 23

Lord, do I not hate those who hate you,
and loathe those who defy you?
I hate them with a total hatred, I regard them
as my own enemies.
Psalm 139:21-22

Isn't it natural, even virtuous, to hate those who hate someone I love? Isn't that simple loyalty? The Bible is full of talk of hatred of those who do not act in accordance with Your will. But You say, "you shall not hate . . . but you shall love your neighbor as yourself." (Lev 19:17-18) Jesus said, "Love your enemies and pray for those who persecute you, so that you may be children of your Father in heaven; for he makes his sun rise on the evil and the good." (Mt 5:44-45) You make your sun rise on the evil and the good in me, as well as the rest of the world. In my gratitude may I act with love, whether I feel like it or not, in the joyful conviction that I am Your child.

February 24

God, examine me and know my heart,
Psalm 139:23(a)

The psalmist is braver than I. Since You know my heart, You know that, like my basement, it's sort of a mess down there: emotions tied to memories I'd rather forget about, cast-off emotions I invested in without thinking, worn-out emotions that I am reluctant to throw away. Who knows? I might want to use them again. But I'd rather You didn't look. I'll sort through it some day, but not now; it's too depressing. But You insist; there is something that You want me to see. Eagerly, You take me by the hand, shining a bright light on all that I want to keep hidden. Look! With the eyes of my heart enlightened, I see the hope to which You call me, the riches of Your glorious inheritance, glowing like treasure among the dusty memories, and my heart is aflame with joy. (Eph 1:18)

February 25

probe me and know my thoughts;
Psalm 139:23(b)

*I*f I were a miner, I might "pierce to the uttermost depths the black and lightless rock." (Job 28:3) If I were an explorer, I could "explore the sources of rivers, and bring to daylight secrets that were hidden." (Job 28:11) But my own thoughts can be hidden and inaccessible to me. Job says that the road to understanding is unknown to every living thing. You alone can probe me and know my thoughts. You alone know the right path to the place of understanding, the place hidden from the eyes of all the living; here, within my heart, where You dwell.

February 26—Emily Malbone Morgan, Prophetic Witness

I do want to say once and for all that if I have had any measure of success in my work, it is I believe due to the fact that I, as a woman, possess the power in common with every other woman of creating a fireside for lonely hearts.[6]

Now as they went on their way, Jesus entered a certain village, where a woman named Martha welcomed him into her home.
Luke 10:38

*A*lthough Jesus chided Martha for complaining that her sister listened to Him instead of helping her, I can't imagine that He didn't appreciate her cooking, serving and cleaning up, a rare treat for the One who had "nowhere to lay his head." (Lk 9:58) Sometimes I feel put-upon and unappreciated for the work I do to make people feel comfortable and cared-for. Emily Malbone Morgan, along with some world-class hostesses in my church, have helped me to see the task of hospitality for the creative, empowering and noble work it is. Next time I feel resentful, help me recall that every day You shower Your loving hospitality on me. Thank You for creating a home for my heart.

---

[6] http://anglicanhistory.org/women/adelynroodsketch.html

February 27

❦

make sure I do not follow pernicious ways,
Psalm 139:24(a)

A way is pernicious when it is subtly harmful or destructive. The serpent was the most subtle of all the animals in the Garden of Eden. (Gen 3:1) The danger is greater because it is not obvious. Eve and Adam allowed the serpent to talk them into following a path that led to their ruin. They wanted to eat the fruit for reasons that sound rational even today: it was good to eat, pleasing to the eye, and desirable for the knowledge it could give. Except that to believe the serpent, they had to also believe that You are a liar. In choosing to follow the serpent's voice, they had to choose not to follow Yours. When beautiful fruit tempts me away from the right path, help me recognize the subtle voice for what it is, and, instead, follow the voice of my Good Shepherd.

February 28—Anna Julia Haywood Cooper, Educator[7]

[F]aith means treating the truth as true. Jesus believed in the infinite possibilities of an individual soul. . . [R]eligion [is] a great deal more than mere gratification of the instinct for worship. Religion must be life made true; and life is action, growth, development--begun now and ending never.[8]

"If you make my word your home you will indeed be my disciples, you will learn the truth and the truth shall make you free."
John 8:31-32

*H*aywood Cooper challenges me to act on Your Word, or, as Jesus says, to make Your Word my home, to live in Your Word. It is a simple goal, but one not easily attained in the face of lies that keep injustice in place. An African-American born enslaved, she did not take the easy way but fought for her right to take courses reserved for men, and, at age 65, became the fourth black woman in American history to earn a PhD. Believing in infinite possibilities, she made her home in Your Word and knew herself to be free, persisting, in spite of seemingly-insurmountable obstacles, to realize her potential to an extent no one but she -- and You -- thought possible. Hers was not an easy life, but a life empowered by Your truth. May I be inspired to meet the challenge of a free life, at home in Your Word.

---

[7] http://en.wikipedia.org/wiki/Anna_Julia_Haywood_Cooper
[8] Cooper, Anna J., A Voice From the South, electronic edition, p. 298-9. http://docsouth.unc.edu/church/cooper/cooper.html#coope127

February 29

and guide me in the way that is everlasting.
Psalm 139:24(b)

*M*y winter retreat comes to an end with the knowledge that the destination is not a place but a way: the way, the truth, and the life, in Jesus. Heaven is not the stereotypical cloud in the sky with angels and nothing to do; heaven is on the road with friends, feeling confused and downcast, discussing everything that has happened, when someone comes near and joins our discussion. His explanations hold us spellbound. At the town, we press Him to stay and eat with us. As He takes the bread, blesses and breaks it, my eyes are opened, and though He vanishes from sight, my heart burns with the conviction that He is risen, and I have arrived.

March:
the Season of Lent —
Answering Wisdom's Call

March 1

✖

On the hilltop, on the road, at the crossways,
Wisdom takes her stand: "To you, O people, I call,
and my cry is to all that live."
Proverbs 8:2,4

Across barriers of time, space, and indifference, Your Spirit calls me into relationship with You: "Hear, O Israel!" (Deut 6:4) Is it a command? an invitation? a plea? Abraham heard Your voice and became a blessing for all the peoples of the earth. (Gen 22:18) The Hebrew people heard Your voice, and, responding with one voice, they became Your own special treasure in covenant relationship with You. (Ex 24:3) At Jesus' Transfiguration the disciples heard Your voice proclaim, "This is my Son, the Beloved. Listen to him!" and they understood, perhaps more than ever before, that they were following the Messiah. (Mk 9:7) During Lent, amidst all the competing claims for my attention, teach me to hear Your voice and respond.

March 2

Listen, I have serious things to tell you,
from my lips come honest words.
Proverbs 8:6

*L*ady Wisdom calls me, but I'm in a hurry right now; I've got things under control. I'll let her know if I need her. But she persists, warning, "If today you hear God's voice, harden not your heart." (Heb 3:7) When Jesus tried to explain to his disciples why He had to die, He asked You to glorify Your name. You spoke, but many of the people who heard You said it was only a clap of thunder, or an angel. Their hearts were hard. Jesus said, "It was not for my sake that this voice came, but for yours." (Jn 12:28-30) When my heart is hard, give me a new heart and a new spirit so that I will hear Your voice and live. (Ezek 36:26)

March 3

The Lord created me when his purpose first unfolded,
before the oldest of his works. When he established the heavens,
I was there, when he drew a circle on the face of the deep.
Proverbs 8:22, 27

*I*n the beginning, Your Spirit hovered over the waters.
(Gen 1:2) Jewish tradition teaches that, not only did
Wisdom exist before creation, she was creation's architect.[1]
I picture You as a sculptor: pondering the clay in Your hand,
ready to begin, excited and anxious to get it right, with Lady
Wisdom hovering at Your shoulder. The March winds blow,
lifting and animating everything in their path. They remind
me that, just as You breathed life into Adam, awakening him
to relationship with You, so the Holy Spirit breathes Christ's
risen life into me, creating me anew to live in relationship
with You.

---

[1] *The Jewish Study Bible,* Oxford University Press, (New York, Oxford University
Press, 2004), p. 1462, n. 30.

March 4

I was by his side, a master craftsman, delighting him
day after day, ever at play in his presence, at play
everywhere in his world, delighting to be
with the sons of men.
Proverbs 8:30-31

This joyful scene shocks me pleasantly out of my too-serious reverie: Lady Wisdom delights to be with me as she playfully assists Your work of creation. I picture children giggling and laughing with her, being recreated in Your image. The snake in the garden has no power to harm those children at play. (Is 11:8) Since my children have grown, I busy myself with task after task after task, postponing play to infrequent, short vacations. This Lent I will give up the false security of constant busyness and heed the playful call of Wisdom.

March 5

*I, Wisdom, am mistress of discretion, the inventor
of lucidity of thought. Good advice and sound judgment
belong to me, perception to me, strength to me.*
Proverbs 8:12, 14

*I*n trying to figure out the right thing to do, I often struggle
alone. If only there were someone who could tell me what
to do! There are those who would listen to my concerns, but
they have concerns of their own and I don't want to burden
them. What if they don't understand? It seems too risky to
ask. The best confidante is totally confidential, totally loving,
and, most importantly, totally on my side, like Miss Taylor
in Jane Austen's *Emma*. Lady Wisdom tells me that when I
have a dilemma, I need look no further than my own heart,
where Your Spirit dwells. She has all the wisdom I could
ever need, if only I am willing to be still and listen.

March 6

I love those who love me; those who seek me eagerly
shall find me.
Proverbs 8:17

*I*n my joy at discovering Lady Wisdom doubts linger. Solomon sings her praises, but are her gifts of discretion, perception, judgment, and strength really for me? Jesus understands my fears and reassures me: "Ask, and it will be given to you; search, and you will find; knock, and the door will be opened to you. For the one who asks always receives; the one who searches always finds; the one who knocks will always have the door opened." (Mt 7:7-8) I sense You waiting patiently behind the door of my pounding heart. "Come," my heart says, "seek His face." (Ps 27:8-9) Hesitantly, I begin to knock.

March 7 — Perpetua and her Companions, Martyrs

"So can I call myself nought other than that which I am, a Christian" [2] *— Perpetua*

I walk in the way of virtue, in the paths of justice.
Proverbs 8:20

Recently catechized, baptized in the face of certain imprisonment, resisting the agonized pleas of her father, with a nursing baby in her arms, Perpetua understood what Dietrich Bonhoeffer called "the cost of discipleship," and walked with firm resolve to a gruesome death.[3] In the earliest surviving text written by a Christian woman, she described her imprisonment and the visions of Your kingdom that sustained her. I am not in danger of persecution for declaring myself a Christian, but perhaps the fear of persecution causes me to avoid certain challenges. Jesus said, "Whoever does not carry the cross and follow me cannot be my disciple." (Lk 14:27) Give me the strength not only to call myself, but to be, a Christian.

---

[2]Medieval Sourcebook: St. Perpetua: *The Passion of Sts. Perpetua and Felicity* (203) http://www.fordham.edu/halsall/source/perpetua.asp

[3] Dietrich Bonhoeffer, *The Cost of Discipleship*, (New York, Touchstone, 1959).

March 8

For wisdom is more precious than pearls, and nothing
else is so worthy of desire.
Proverbs 8:11

*K*ing Solomon, famous for his wealth, prized wisdom above all things: "compared with her, I held riches as nothing. I reckoned no priceless stone to be her peer." (Wis 7:8-9) Solomon fell in love with wisdom as with a bride; knowing that with her alone would he find joy, he prayed for her with all his heart. (Wis 8:2, 16) In return, You gave him wisdom greater than that of anyone, with breadth of understanding as vast as the sand on the seashore. (1 Kings 4:29) Were there pearls of wisdom hidden beneath those sands? Could she be the hidden treasure, my pearl of great price? (Mt 13:45-46)

March 9

Happy those who keep my ways!
Happy the one who listens to me, watching
daily at my gates, waiting beside my doors.
Proverbs 8:32, 34

*D*ay after day, I wake up and rush to get ready, but for what? I prepare, but for whom? Behind the door of my heart, You wait patiently for me to knock, and where am I? Rushing off to do something more urgent. I don't have time to pray right now. You understand; I have to get some things done before I can think about being happy. "Her ways are delightful ways, her paths all lead to contentment." (Prov 3:17) What am I looking for, if not joy and contentment? Who are all my strivings for, if not for You?

March 10

For the one who finds me finds life, and
will win favor from the Lord.
Proverbs 8:35

*A*fter being tempted in the desert, Jesus, filled with the power of Your Spirit, went to the synagogue in Nazareth to read, "The Spirit of the Lord is upon me, because he has anointed me to bring good news to the poor. He has sent me to proclaim release to the captives and recovery of sight to the blind, to let the oppressed go free, to proclaim the year of the Lord's favor." Then He said, "Today this scripture has been fulfilled in your hearing." (Lk 4:13-21) Your Spirit empowered Jesus to proclaim that life in Your kingdom is here and now. Good news for the poor, healing, and liberation from slavery of every kind, are, through Jesus, a present reality. Through the Spirit of the risen Christ, I have been given life to the full, free from the bondage of sin and death. Through the Spirit, I have won Your favor.

March 11

❧

Those who acquire Wisdom win God's friendship.
Wisdom 7:14

How amazing to think that I could be Your friend! Even more amazing: You want to be my friend! I feel like a schoolgirl, thrilled and gratified beyond words to have won a relationship so necessary and so rare. With friendship comes the security of knowing I am loved; I can withstand the hurts of life. But how do I know whether I have acquired Wisdom sufficient to win that prize? I have Jesus' assurance that through Him, I have received what is necessary. "I call you friends, because I have made known to you everything I have learned from my Father." (Jn 15:15) What could You want from me? What does any friend want from another?

March 12

Within her is a spirit intelligent, holy, unique, manifold,
subtle, active, incisive, unsullied,
lucid, invulnerable, benevolent, sharp, . . .
Wisdom 7:22

*W*ho knew that Lady Wisdom was so variously endowed with virtues, like a diamond with many facets reflecting the brilliance of Your Spirit? Who could comprehend the multitude of gifts contained within that radiance, each beam of which could transfix for days of gazing? The more I learn about Lady Wisdom, the more I want to explore this "inexhaustible treasure." (Wis 7:14) Her riches are too many to grasp, yet there is more . . .

March 13

. . . irresistible, beneficent, loving, steadfast, dependable,
unperturbed, almighty, all-surveying,
penetrating all intelligent, pure and most subtle spirits.
Wisdom 7:23

*L*ady Wisdom sounds too good to be true. How could all the assistance I need be mine for the asking? "Watch for her early and you will have no trouble; be on the alert for her and anxiety will quickly leave you." (Wis 6:14-15) What's the catch? In the headlong rush to get things done it is not so easy to stop and listen. I have to give up being right and admit that my judgment about what to do and how to do it might not be the best. I must choose between my desire to be in control, with the familiar feeling of anxiety, and my desire to be wise, with a measure of peace. Which will I choose?

March 14

Wisdom is quicker to move than any motion;
she is so pure, she pervades and permeates all things.
Wisdom 7:24

*I*n You I live and move and have my being. (Acts 17:28) Space and time are Your creations. They form the continuum of salvation history along which I journey within Your kingdom, guided by Lady Wisdom. Unlimited by the laws of physics, she travels freely, blowing where she will. Relative to her, space and time are the crude but necessary vehicles that convey me, via the wormhole of grace, safely past the black holes of ignorance and fear, to where? I cannot know the destination, but, borne by Your Spirit, I am happy to be along for the ride.

March 15

※

She is a breath of the power of God,
pure emanation of the glory of the Almighty.
Wisdom 7:25(a)

The theologian and mystic, Hildegaard of Bingen,[4] said this of her own legendary singing:

> Listen: there was once a king sitting on
> his throne. It pleased the king to raise a
> small feather from the ground, and he
> commanded it to fly. The feather flew,
> not because of anything in itself but because
> the air bore it along. Thus am I, a feather on
> the breath of God."[5]

Borne on Your breath in aural ecstasy, Hildegaard revealed Your glory. I long to feel Your wind beneath my wings; let me float and fly!

---

[4] *See* September 17.
[5] http://elvis.rowan.edu/~kilroy/jek/09/17.html

March 16

She is a reflection of the eternal light, untarnished mirror
of God's active power, image of his goodness.
Wisdom 7:26

Your work is not finished yet. Creation is ongoing, as You continue to incarnate Your glory on earth, one person at a time. Your Spirit frees me to see Your glory as though reflected in a mirror; thus I am transformed "from one degree of glory to another." (2 Cor 3:18) Lady Wisdom, image of Your goodness, aids Your good work in me: reflecting You, mirroring Your power, dazzling my unveiled eyes, and transforming me into the person You created me to be.

March 17

Although alone, she can do all; herself unchanging,
she makes all things new.
Wisdom 7:27

*L*ike the mythical supermom, Lady Wisdom can do it all. Can she make a new me? Can she give me work that is fun, satisfying, and fairly paid? Children who call me? Friends who are always at hand when I need them? No? St. Paul says that those who are in Christ are a new creation; everything old has passed away and become new. (2 Cor 5:17) At my baptism, she hovered over the waters in which I became a new creation, a member of Christ's body. It is up to me to discover and enjoy this gift of new life in Christ.

March 18

In each generation she passes into holy souls,
she makes them friends of God and prophets.
Wisdom 7:27

I am privileged to have known a few of those holy souls. They don't look unusual but they are: deeper, more reflective, more empathic; yes, wiser. They know You. Although they are not famous, people are drawn to them as to a magnet. They are not happier than other people, rather the opposite, yet joy is in them, and the peace that passes all understanding. These few have been my companions through the dark valley. Step by difficult step, they walked with me, bringing me ever closer to You. There are not words to express my gratitude to them, although I have tried. The only thanks possible are to turn to the next person and offer them my hand as we answer Wisdom's call.

March 19

She is indeed more splendid than the sun,
she outshines all the constellations; compared with light,
she takes first place, for light must yield to night,
but over Wisdom evil can never triumph.
Wisdom 7:29

Lady Wisdom, emanation of Your glory, outshines the brightest lights imaginable. She is light of another quality entirely: not only visual but tangible; of the senses and yet transcendent; light unbounded by time or space; light to which darkness is not dark, against which evil cannot stand. She is the original Light, the Light of Christ, "a light that darkness could not overpower," (Jn 1:5) the Light within which I am, even now, united with You and all creation in Your kingdom.

March 20

She deploys her strength from one end of the earth
to the other, ordering all things for good.
Wisdom 8:1

Some say everything happens for a reason, implying that pain and loss are somehow part of Your master plan. Jesus tells a different story: "I have come that you may have life and have it to the full." (Jn 10:10[b]) Evil is a reality that Your Spirit has conquered already, and not yet. Wisdom orders all things toward an ultimate good: the parousia, the time when You will be all in all. My job is not to figure out when and how that will happen, but only to cooperate with You in Your plan for the full communion of all creation with You. Let it be done in me according to Your will.

March 21

Her closeness to God lends luster to her noble birth,
since the Lord of All has loved her.
Wisdom 8:3

On the sixth day of creation You said, "Let us make man in our own image, in the likeness of ourselves. . . ." You—plural —created humankind in Your own image, male and female. (Gen 1:26-27) You, complete in Yourself, somehow need creatures to reflect Your feminine Self. It's marvelous to think that I am descended from Your beloved Lady Wisdom, she who was Your helpmate at the dawn of creation. You knew from experience that Adam needed Eve. His exclamation, "This last is bone of my bones, flesh of my flesh," speaks of a visceral recognition; of a relief, joyous and heartfelt; of a longing no less deep for being unknown until that moment. (Gen 2:23)

March 22

She is an initiate in the mysteries of God's knowledge,
making choice of the works he is to do.
Wisdom 8:4

*I*n the ancient world, participation in mysteries was reserved to initiates who could not reveal cult secrets to outsiders.[6] Here, Lady Wisdom is described as such an initiate, privy to Your secrets as no human could be. Nevertheless, Paul, in his letter to the Ephesians, makes this startling claim: that You have made known to us the mystery of Your will, in Christ, as a plan for the fullness of time, to gather up all things in Him, in heaven and on earth. (Eph 1:9-10) Jesus said, "nothing is secret that will not become known." What I have heard in the dark, I will tell in the light; what I hear whispered, I will proclaim from the housetops. (Mt 10:26-27)

---

[6] http://en.wikipedia.org/wiki/Greco-Roman_mysteries

March 23

She understands what is pleasing in your eyes and
what agrees with your commandments.
Wisdom 9:9(b)

What is Your will for me? How can I be faithful? These are ancient questions to which there have been myriad answers, but who could know Your mind? There are Your commandments, but how to live them out is not always easy to know. Lady Wisdom knows, and the prophets, and Jesus. It turns out that the answer is not complicated:

> *What is good has been explained to you;*
> *this is what the Lord asks of you:*
> *only this, to act justly,*
> *to love tenderly*
> *and to walk humbly with your God. (Mic 6:8)*

March 24

Send her forth from your throne of glory to help me.
Wisdom 9:10

𝐹rom the beginning of salvation history, You sent Lady Wisdom to guide Your people. The image of Your faithfulness, she did not abandon them, but led them out of slavery into freedom in covenant relationship with You. (Wis 10) You incarnated Your Self in Jesus, Your Word, "the true light that enlightens all people," and sent Him forth to manifest Your glory so humbly here on earth. (Jn 1:9, 14) After His death and resurrection, He did not abandon Your people but sent the Spirit of truth to lead them out of bondage to sin and death, to live freely in intimate relationship with You. Can I doubt that Your Spirit is guiding me, too? And yet I do doubt. Jesus says all things can be done for the one who believes. I believe; help my unbelief! (Mk 9:23-24)

March 25

🪬

She herself walks about looking for those who are worthy
of her and graciously shows herself to them as they go,
in every thought of theirs coming to meet them.
Wisdom 6:16-17

The Book of Wisdom names many men found worthy of
Lady Wisdom's aid, and not one woman. (Wis 10) Yet one
woman was found worthy of partnering with You in salvation
history: Mary. You walked with Adam, You talked with
Abraham and Moses, and You wrestled with Jacob. With
Mary You conceived a child. Your work with Adam, Noah
and the rest of them was a *fait accompli;* You proclaimed Your
will and they obeyed. Before the birth of Christ, through
Mary, a entirely new relationship was born between You
and all humanity. Mary was weak and You are mighty, yet
You humbly asked her consent to bear the Messiah. She
responded not in fear but nobly, declaring herself to be Your
handmaid. Before Jesus showed humanity what You can be,
Mary showed what humanity is called to be.

March 26

She will guide me prudently in my undertakings
and protect me by her glory.
Wisdom 9:11

𝒴our Glory is not an ineffable something "up there," but the way You assure me of Your presence. When You led the Hebrew people through the wilderness, Your glory shone in the pillars of cloud and fire. (Ex 13:21) On Sinai, You appeared to Moses in a dense cloud so that the people could see Your glory, hear You speak, and learn to trust you always. (Ex 19:9) At the Transfiguration, when Jesus appeared on the mountain with Moses and Elijah, Your glory overshadowed them in a bright cloud, and the disciples heard Your voice. (Mt 17:2-5) Today, I hear Your voice in the Word; in the eucharist I receive Your glory: the fire in the bread and the glow in the wine. [7]

---

[7] Griffith, Sidney H., "'Spirit in the Bread; Fire in the Wine': the Eucharist as 'Living Medicine' in the Thought of Ephraem the Syrian," *Modern Theology* 15:2 April 1999.

March 27

*And so I prayed, and understanding was given to me;
I entreated, and the spirit of Wisdom came to me.*
Wisdom 7:7

This Lenten season, I have learned that wisdom means hearing Your voice, and then taking a leap of faith. Jesus says ask and I will receive. (Mt 7:7-8) Is it really that easy? All I need to do to receive wisdom and understanding is ask — and give up some control. Why should that be so frightening? Nearing the edge of the cliff, dizzy and a little queasy, I am afraid to jump. Please, please, please be there! But You are not there, You are here. I called, and You came to me.

March 28

*As for your intention, who could have learned it,
had you not granted Wisdom and sent your
holy spirit from above?*
Wisdom 9:17

*I*t is difficult to accept that the most solid thing in my life
is invisible, and yet, through painful and frightening times,
I have found it to be true. "What no eye has seen, nor ear
heard, nor the human heart conceived," those things which
You have prepared for me are the most real. (1 Cor 2:9-10)
Had You not sent Your Spirit, Your gifts of the Bible, liturgy,
and the sacraments would be mere words and empty gestures.
Through Christ's death and resurrection, they become the
means by which You breathe Your life into me, just as You
breathed life into Adam; and by which You enflesh Yourself
in me, as You enfleshed Yourself in Eve. In the liturgy, I
inhale Your breath of life so that I may breathe that Life back
to You in all I do.

March 29

Wisdom has built herself a house, she has erected her seven pillars.
Proverbs 9:1

From hilltop and crossroads, Lady Wisdom cries out to all who live, calling them to a particular time and place: the eucharist. There, she has built Your house of prayer for all peoples. There, I receive Your Word, so that Your joy may be in me and my joy may be complete. (Jn 15:11) Supported by Wisdom's seven pillars, the sacraments, I am reborn, marked as Your own forever, and nourished with Your very self. Wisdom says, "Come." And let everyone who hears say, "Come." And let everyone who is thirsty come. Let anyone who wishes take the water of life as a gift. (Rev 22:17)

March 30

✠

She has slaughtered her beasts, prepared her wine,
she has laid her table.
Proverbs 9:2

Slowly, methodically, patiently, over unimaginable eons of time, You prepared Your table. You created light and dark; waters and dry land; vegetation; sun, moon, and stars; sea creatures, birds, and beasts: all was good, and yet something was missing. You created man and woman in Your own image; it was very good, and still, something was missing. Existence is a gift, but what is existence without relationship? And what is relationship without celebration? And so You have prepared a banquet, the eucharist, at which the marriage of heaven and earth in Christ is recreated and celebrated; a foretaste of that heavenly banquet of rich food and well-aged wines, when You will be all in all. (Is 25:6) There, my patient, forgiving Father, You await me with open arms.

March 31

She has dispatched her maidservants and
proclaimed from the city's heights:
"Come and eat my bread, drink the wine I have prepared!"
Proverbs 9:3, 5

*A*s the rain comes down from heaven and does not return to
You without watering the earth, making it yield and provide
seed for the sower and bread for the hungry, so Your Word
does not return to You empty, without carrying out Your will
and succeeding in what it was sent to do. (Is 55:10-11) Thus,
the Word became flesh and dwelt among us (Jn 1:14), and at
the Last Supper, He took bread, blessed and broke it, saying,
"Take it and eat; this is my body." Then he took a cup of wine
and said, "Drink all of you from this, for this is my blood, the
blood of the covenant, which is to be poured out for many
for the forgiveness of sins." (Mt 26:26-28) In His memory, I
eat and drink, returning like rain to You.

April:
the Season of Easter:
Experiencing Resurrection
Here and Now

April 1

*"Go you forth from your land, from your kindred,
from your father's house to the land that I will let you see.
I will make a great nation of you and will give you blessing
and will make your name great. Be a blessing!"*
Genesis 12:1-2

*R*esurrection is a blessing that begins with death: the new plant arises from the death of the seed; the butterfly arises from the death of the caterpillar; the Hebrew people arose from the death of Abraham's former way of life; the new life of Christ arose from the death of Jesus. Those deaths were real, yet life was not snuffed out. Rather, in some mysterious way, life was preserved and exploded into something unimaginably greater and more beautiful. In baptism, I died to sin and death and rose again to new life in Christ. During this season of Easter, help me live into the gift of resurrection; help me be a blessing.

April 2

"I will bless her, and I will give you a son from her,
I will bless her so that she becomes nations,
kings of peoples shall come from her!"
Genesis 17:16

Sara was not merely the biological means for the fulfillment of Your blessing, she shared your blessing with Abraham and herself became a blessing. You transformed Sara into Sarah, a new creation; from her came another new creation, the Hebrew people.[1] Your Holy Spirit transformed Mary into the mother of God. From her came Christ, in whom all humanity became a new creation. (2 Cor 5:17) In baptism, You blessed me and made me a new creation: Your own daughter. I am not Sara or Mary, yet you call me to be a blessing for the world. What new creation is gestating in me, waiting to be born?

---

[1] *The Five Books of Moses, The Schocken Bible, Vol. I,* Everett Fox, ed. (New York, Schocken Books, 1995), p. 73, nn. 15 and 16.

April 3

Then David blessed the Lord in the presence of all the assembly;
David said: "Blessed are you, O Lord, the God of our
ancestor Israel, forever and ever."
1 Chronicles 29:10

Growing up, I never thought that a person could bless You. How could a human being bless You, who are complete and all-powerful? You don't need or want anything. Or so I thought. *I* need, *I* want, therefore I pray, and You deliver. Isn't that how it works? Much later in life I began to understand that You do indeed want, even need, something from me beyond obedience. Covenant, old or new, is just another word for a committed relationship. You love me and bless me, and, just like any other lover or loving parent, You want very much that I will love and bless You in return.

April 4

𝍢

Blessed are you, O Lord; teach me your statutes.
Psalm 119:12

$\mathcal{A}$s a child I learned the Ten Commandments, or Decalogue, as a list of things that I must not do, on penalty of death -- a very limited view that casts You in the very limited role of judge. Unconstrained by human expectations, You led Your people to freedom from slavery for a new kind of life in relationship with You: "I will take you as my people, and I will be your God. You shall know that I am the Lord your God, who has freed you from the burdens of the Egyptians." (Ex 6:7) Unlike the gods of that time, You gave the Decalogue, the Ten Words, with no word of punishment, [2] unburdening Your people so that they could don Your light yoke and learn from You. (Mt 11:29-30) Far from inhibiting my life, Your teachings free me to be a blessing.

---

[2] *The Five Books of Moses*, p. 368.

April 5 — Pandita Mary Ramabai, Prophetic Witness and Evangelist [3]

"My girls and I are quite ready to forego all our comforts . .
. and live as plainly as we can. [S]o long as we have a little
room or a seed of grain left in this house,
we shall try and help our sisters who are starving." [4]

Those who are generous are blessed, for they
share their bread with the poor.
Proverbs 22:9

*H*ow could it be a blessing to share one's last bit of food? Just thinking about it makes me feel fearful, yet Pandita Ramabai describes her life as full of joy, love, and contentment, as well as trials and difficulties. Not knowing where the money would come from, she set out to rescue 300 starving girls and women who had been abandoned by their families. Anticipating the challenges ahead she wrote: "If all of us do our part faithfully, God is faithful to fulfill His promises, and will send us the help we need at this time." She became a blessing, not only for the 300, but for all child widows in India. Could I be such a blessing? Could there be a joy deeper, a satisfaction greater for me?

---

[3] http://en.wikipedia.org/wiki/Pandita_Mary_Ramabai
[4] Helen S Dyer, *Pandita Ramabai: the Story of Her Life,* (Fleming H. Revell Co., 1900) , p. 104.

April 6

Blessed are those who trust in the Lord,
whose trust is the Lord.
Jeremiah 17:7

The scripture presents two ways to become a blessing, using the same word but in different ways. In the first phrase trust is a verb; in the second, trust is a noun and is equated with You. Jesus does not use the word *trust* in the gospels; in fact, *trust* is used only once in the New Testament, in the first letter of Peter who says that through Jesus we have come to trust in You. (1 Pet 1:21) Jesus does not ask his disciples to trust You; instead he says, "Do not fear, only believe." (Mk 5:36) If You *are* trust I am relieved of the effort of trusting; if I believe in You, trust is mine and fear is irrelevant —blessing indeed! The father of a sick child said to Jesus, "I believe; help my unbelief!" It was enough; Jesus healed that child. Through Christ You are my trust, and I am blessed.

April 7

*Blessed be the name of God from age to age,
for wisdom and power are his.*
Daniel 2:20

Your name is not like any other name. When You asked Moses to lead the Children of Israel out of Egypt, Moses said, "Here, I will come to the Children of Israel and I will say to them: The God of your fathers has sent me to you, and they will say to me: What is his name? — what shall I say to them?" You answered, "I will be-there howsoever I will be-there. Thus shall you say to the Children of Israel: I-Will-Be-There sends me." [5] (Ex 3:14) No mere title, Your name is an active presence, a living blessing that dwells in the midst of Your people. (Ex 25:8) When Jesus was born, Your name became flesh and dwelled among us (Jn 1:14), a living blessing that death could not restrain. In Christ's risen life You are: there, here and everywhere; then, now and always.

---

[5] *The Five Books of Moses,* p. 273.

April 8

*"Blessed are the poor in spirit, for theirs is the
kingdom of heaven."*
Matthew 5:3

*I*n the Sermon on the Mount, Jesus describes the meaning
of "Thy kingdom come, Thy will be done, on earth as it is
in heaven," with uncomfortable specificity. No gospel
of abundance here. Your blessings are not prizes to be
won; rather, the state of grace is an uncomfortable place
of vulnerability. The poor in spirit, the downtrodden, the
physically or mentally handicapped: these own the kingdom
that Jesus said is like yeast that a woman took and mixed
with three measures of flour until all of it was leavened.
(Mt 13:33) In the kingdom of heaven the poor in spirit
become a blessing. Acting as leaven for the world, they
provoke a rising up, releasing an unseen force that causes
humanity to grow.

April 9

✠

"Blessed are you who are poor, for yours is the
kingdom of God."
Luke 6:20

*W*hat is this kingdom that the poor possess, in which they are a blessing? It is a place in which a mustard seed, tiny as dust, is changed by a mysterious force hidden within and transformed into a blessing that shelters the birds of the air. (Lk 13:18-19) Nearly inaccessible for the wealthy (Lk 18:25), the kingdom may be entered by one who receives it as a little child. (Lk 18:17) The poor possess as a gift from You a rich faith that transforms their insignificance into shelter for Your kingdom in the world. (Jam 2:5) Riches obscure the poverty of my faith, yet the mysterious force within the seed grows within me as well, with the power to transform my poverty into a blessing. (Lk 17:21)

April 10

*"Blessed are those who mourn, for they
will be comforted."*
Matthew 5:4

*I*n the synagogue Jesus read, "The Spirit of the Lord God is upon me, because the Lord has sent me to comfort all who mourn; to provide for those who mourn in Zion -- to give them . . . the oil of gladness instead of mourning, the mantle of praise instead of a faint spirit." (Is 61:1, 3) The repetition of the word *mourn* shows how acutely You felt the suffering of Your people. You sent Jesus to comfort those who mourn, yet His own words speak of comfort as a future blessing. In preparing the disciples for His death, Jesus told them that only if He died could the Holy Spirit come and turn their pain to joy. (Jn 16:7, 20-22) Jesus had to die in order to rise again and become a blessing to all those who mourn, regardless of time and place. Help me remember that the past must die, and I must mourn, before the present can become a joyous blessing.

April 11

"Blessed are you who weep now, for you will laugh."
Luke 6:21(b)

*I*n Your kingdom, unlike an earthly kingdom, the usual rules of power are reversed. In Your kingdom power does not oppress some for the benefit of others, but heals all. (Lk 6:19) In Your kingdom, those who suffer under the powerful of this world are blessed; those who thrive under the conditions that create that suffering mourn and weep. (Lk 6:25) In your kingdom the measure I give, expecting nothing in return, is the measure I get back, pressed down, shaken together, running over. (Lk 6:38) By whose measure do I give? By whose rules do I live?

April 12

✵

"Blessed are the meek, for they will inherit the earth."
Matthew 5:5

The meek are quiet, gentle, easily imposed upon and submissive. Surely, no one would be meek if they could help it, yet Jesus says the meek will inherit the earth! Just as Your kingdom is not like an earthly kingdom, Your power is not like human power. When Jesus stood before Pilate, Pilate asked Him, "Are you the King of the Jews?" Jesus replied that His kingdom is not of this world; if His kingdom were from this world, His followers would be fighting to keep Him from being handed over. (Jn 18:36) Though Jesus was Your Son, He submitted defenseless to the power of this world, allowing Himself to be led like a lamb to slaughter. (Phil 2:5-10) By His submission He inherited all things in heaven and on earth. (Eph 1:10) When I feel attacked, what power will I use? What power will best enable me to be a blessing?

April 13

"Blessed are those who hunger and thirst for righteousness,
for they will be filled."
Matthew 5:6

*I*n the Exodus, the Hebrew people had to discover that their hunger and thirst could not be satisfied by the fleshpots of slavery, that You are the source of nourishment. Patiently You fed them on manna as they slowly learned to walk as free people. In the desert You slaked their thirst with water struck from a rock, striking new life from their slavery-hardened hearts. "Oh, come to the water all you who are thirsty! Listen to me and you will have good things to eat. Come to me, and your soul will live!" (Is 55:1-3) Four thousand people came to listen to Jesus, some of them from a great distance, and he did not want to send them away with nothing to eat. How could anyone get bread in such a deserted place? Jesus blessed a few loaves and fish and they ate their fill. (Mk 8:1-9) My hunger and thirst are blessings that open my heart to be filled by You.

April 14

✤

"Blessed are you who are hungry now,
for you will be filled. "
Luke 6:21(a)

There is hunger that is metaphoric and there is hunger that is literal: stark, hellish, a shocking abomination. This hunger is not a blessing. After the resurrection, Jesus appeared to the disciples on the shore of the lake where they were fishing without success. He suggested putting their net to starboard and there were so many fish they could not haul it in. They realized it was He and hurried to shore. In the breaking light they saw bread and a charcoal fire with fish cooking on it. Jesus said, "Come and have breakfast." Afterward, Jesus said to Peter, "Do you love me?" and Peter answered, "Yes, Lord, you know I love you." Jesus said, "Feed my lambs." Jesus repeated three times, "Do you love me?" then "Feed my sheep." (Jn 21) While I sometimes wonder what Your will is for me, this task is clear.

April 15

"Blessed are the merciful, for they will receive mercy."
Matthew 5:7

*E*ven in Your kingdom, I'd like to think there are a few simple formulas for living. This beatitude is just another version of the Golden Rule: treat others as I would have them treat me. Simple, right? But mercy cannot be reduced to a simple law of karma. From the beginning of your covenant relationship with the Hebrew people, mercy was no less than the meeting place between heaven and earth.[6] Jesus incarnated Your presence on earth, embodying Your mercy in order to free me from sin and death, confounding human calculations of cause and effect. When I am merciful, I embody Your mercy on earth as it is in heaven. No longer isolated, my act of mercy is giving that becomes receiving that becomes giving, in an endless chain of blessing.

---

[6] *The Five Books of Moses,* p. 401, n. 22.

April 16 —Mary Brant Konwatsijayenni, Witness to the Faith

Mary Brant was an evangelist and leader of the Mohawk native American tribe. The prayer for today is an excerpt from her memoirs, written in 1796.

Blessed be the God and Father of our Lord Jesus Christ! By his great mercy he has given us a new birth into a living hope through the resurrection of Jesus Christ from the dead.
1 Peter 1:3

"There are many transitions in life. Change is complex and usually difficult. Jesus speaks to troubled hearts. He tells them they know the way. They don't feel like they know the way. Look at Jesus. He is the way. Or hear his words. They speak of the way. Or see his works. They point the way. Love one another. The Spirit abides in you.

"So we remember who and whose we are. We remind ourselves that the present wilderness and threat is better than the former bondage and ignorance. Life is difficult. We are always on the way. But Jesus is the journey and the journey's end. It seems that he believes in us. That may be more important than our believing in him. He thinks we can not only survive but prevail. He tells us that we will do the works that he does, and even more. He invites us to imagine, and to ask, and to act. We have an Advocate. A Spirit with us. Come on. Let's go." [7]

— Mary Brant Konwatsijayenni

---

[7] http://www.saintnicks.com/news_article.php?id=1197&search=0

April 17

❧

"Blessed rather are those who hear the
word of God and obey it!"
Luke 11:28

This statement by Jesus was prompted by the exclamation of
a woman in the crowd listening to Him, "Blessed is the womb
that bore you and the breasts that nursed you!" Jesus knew
that His wisdom and power were not the result of having a
particular mother, that His was not a human achievement.
Jesus' reminder that Your word, and not His mother, was His
source of nourishment, reminds me that the same source of
nourishment that enabled Him to do Your will enables me
as well. Jesus didn't say, "worship me," He said, "Follow me."
Worshipping Jesus is beside the point, unless it leads me to
heed Your word and become a blessing.

April 18

"Blessed are you when people revile you and persecute
you and utter all kinds of evil against you falsely on my account.
Rejoice and be glad, for your reward is great in heaven,
for in the same way they persecuted the
prophets who were before you"
Matthew 5:11-12

*I*n a time when some religious orders were very worldly, Teresa of Avila worked to found a convent devoted to contemplative prayer. Beset by persecution, she complained to Jesus about the hostility and gossip that surrounded her. He said, "Teresa, that's how I treat my friends" and Teresa responded, "No wonder you have so few friends." [8] It is a mystery why, even now, a determined effort toward You can encounter so much resistance. Perhaps, as in Teresa's day, no one wants to be reminded of the way that You want them to live. So what is there to rejoice about? For Teresa, prayer was "an intimate sharing between friends," an experience of heaven on earth that far outweighed her suffering. When my best efforts encounter resistance, help me remember that time spent with You is always a blessing.

---

[8] http://www.catholic.org/saints/saint.php?saint_id=208

April 19

Blessed is she who believed that there would be a
fulfillment of what was spoken to her by the Lord.
Luke 1:45

*W*hen the angel asked Mary to become the mother of
Your Son, Jesus, she was greatly troubled and pondered what
the angel's greeting could mean. In spite of her incredulity
and fear, she said "yes." Was she happy? Luke doesn't tell us
how she felt as she traveled to visit her cousin, Elizabeth,
who was six months pregnant in her old age. The meaning
of the word *blessed* in the Bible varies. Here, blessed means
the happiness that results from being favored by You.[9] The
happiness of Elizabeth and Mary was a manifestation of
Your Spirit's presence both within and among them, a sign
that Your kingdom had come. (Lk 15:7, 9, 22-24) Today, I
will believe in Your word and share my belief with another,
so that together we may taste the joy of life in Your kingdom.

---

[9] William J. Urbrock, "Blessings and Curses," in ABD, ed. David Noel
Freedman, vol. 1 (New York; London: Doubleday and Company, 1992) p. 756.

April 20

"Blessed are those slaves whom the master finds alert when he comes; truly I tell you, he will fasten his belt and have them sit down to eat, and he will come and serve them."
Luke 12:37

*I*t appears from some of His statements that Jesus thought that the end of the world was very near, yet He died and rose again, appeared to the disciples, and life went on. The world won't come to an end if I don't pray every day; I know that from experience. How important is it for me to remain alert? What could happen? Earthquakes big and small, fast- and slow-moving, come into my life unbidden. Suddenly, it seems, I'm overwhelmed and on my knees begging for help. I wonder if You get tired of this routine. Imagine how things might be different if I checked in with You every day, alert and attuned to Your voice. When the world comes to an end—it has before and it will again—I will not panic. I will call, and You will answer; I shall cry for help and You will say, "Here I am." (Is 58:9)

April 21

"No servant is greater than the master,
no messenger is greater than the one who sent him.
Now that you know this, happiness will be yours
if you behave accordingly."
John 13:16-17

In my years of working in children's religious formation, I have had much happiness, and also frustration in encountering various obstacles: some expected, like finding child care; some unexpected, like lack of support from parents and clergy. When I find myself wondering why it is so difficult to do Your work, I tell myself, why should I have it any easier than Jesus? The parables tell us that while the kingdom of heaven is incredibly valuable and precious, it is also small and hidden. Give me the grace to make my peace with servanthood and be a blessing.

April 22

※

"Blessed are those who have not seen and
yet have come to believe."
John 20:29

"Who is luckier? Those who walked with Jesus or those of us who are alive today?" I asked the 6, 7, and 8 year-olds in front of me. Opinions varied. Who wouldn't want to walk with Jesus, to see His face, to hear His voice or feel the touch of His hand? In comparison, belief in His risen life seems a cold, abstract concept. On the other hand, there is no earthly life without death. When Jesus died, His disciples were engulfed in grief and fear; their life with Him seemed over—until they saw the risen Christ. I have never experienced Christ's human presence but His risen life is physically present to me in the word and in the bread and wine. The Good Shepherd is with me always. I need only be still and listen; soon, I hear that beloved voice calling me by name and I am blessed with a joy that can never be taken away from me.

April 23

*"Blessed are those whose iniquities are forgiven,
and whose sins are covered."*
Romans 4:7

*W*hen Jesus saw the paralyzed man, He said, "Take heart, son, your sins are forgiven." (Mt 9:2) It seems a curious thing to say when it was obvious that the man couldn't walk. But Your Son, like You, sees beyond physical appearances to the heart. (1 Sam 16:7) There is a paralysis more profound than physical paralysis. The heaviness of guilt consciously or unconsciously weighs down the soul, like irons fastened onto the legs of a convict in earlier times. The spirit, buried beneath its sins, cannot rise. When I am prostrate and a long way off, my Father sees me and is moved with pity. He runs to me, clasps me in His arms, covers my sins with the best robe, and invites me to the banquet. (Lk 15:20-23) At the eucharistic feast, freed from the bondage of sin, I rise to new life; I become a blessing.

April 24

꧁꧂

Those who believe are blessed with Abraham who believed.
Galatians 3:8–9

Because Abraham put his faith in You, in him all the nations of the earth are blessed. When I put my faith in You I inherit Your blessing through Abraham, my father in faith. What is the blessing that Abraham received, that I inherit from him? Children? I have a couple. Land? I have a little. Fame? I have none. Whatever I imagine this blessing to be, it is beyond imagining: "Look up to the heavens and count the stars if you can." (Gen 15:5) Yours is not an earthly kingdom. At once vast, encompassing the heavens and the earth; and minute, existing within the smallest seed on earth; eternal, yet here and now; hidden, yet precious beyond measure. Many will gather from east and west to eat with Abraham, Isaac and Jacob in that kingdom, at that table to which I, too, am invited to be blessed. (Mt 8:11)

April 25

In returning and rest you shall be saved; in quietness and in trust shall be your strength.
For the Lord is a God of justice; blessed are all those who wait for him.
Isaiah 30:15, 18

Having been a doormat for much of my life, it has been important for me not to be passive in a crisis, but to assert myself, albeit peacefully. Here, Isaiah tells Israel that her salvation lays in conversion and tranquility, her strength in complete trust in You, rather than self-reliance. Jesus said, "Unless you change and become like children, you will never enter the kingdom of heaven." (Mt 18:3) When I am in crisis, the question whether to be passive or assertive is a distraction from the fundamental question of whether I will rely on myself alone or trust You to assist me. Self-reliance is tempting; it's the devil I know. When I rely on You, I can rest; I can be quiet, "as a child in its mother's arms, as content as a child that has been weaned." (Ps 131:2) From that place of security comes strength and the ability to be a blessing, even in a crisis.

April 26

❧

Blessed is the one who reads aloud the words of the prophecy,
and blessed are those who hear and who keep
what is written in it; for the time is near.
Revelation 1:3

Prophecy, the secrets that You want everyone to know, is powerful; powerful enough to raise the dead. You set Ezekiel down in a valley filled with dry bones, and told him to prophesy to them, "Say, 'Dry bones hear the word of the Lord. I am now going to make the breath to enter you, and you shall live.'" You said, "Prophesy to the breath, 'The Lord says this: Come from the four winds, breath, breathe on these dead; let them live!'" Ezekiel prophesied as You ordered him, breath entered the bones and they came to life. (Ezek 37:4-10) The Hebrew word for breath, *ruach*, also means spirit. When I read Your word aloud, new life springs from lifeless pages and resurrection happens. Filled with Your Spirit, my arid places come alive and I become a blessing.

April 27 — Christina Rossetti, Poet

My life is like a faded leaf, My harvest dwindled to a husk:
Truly my life is void and brief and tedious in the barren dusk;
My life is like a frozen thing, No bud nor greenness can I see:
Yet rise it shall—the sap of Spring; O Jesus, rise in me.[10]

"Blessed are the pure in heart, for they will see God."
Matthew 5:8

What does it mean to be pure in heart? The psalmist says, "I look to no one else in heaven, I delight in nothing else on earth." (Ps 73:25) Who but a saint can be so single-minded, thinking only of You? My feet are made of clay; my thoughts stray. Christina Rossetti contemplated the emptiness of her life with faith in the resurrection. Comparing herself with nature in winter, she believed that her heart, like the dead seed, contained the source of new life. My life may seem dry, faded, tedious, or barren, yet the life of the risen Christ, the sap in the true vine, flows through me. Spring, like resurrection, always comes, and I will know myself to be a blessing.

---

[10] excerpt from "A Better Resurrection," by Christina Rosetti, http://www.poetryfoundation.org/poem/174257

April 28

"Come, you that are blessed by my Father,
inherit the kingdom prepared for you
from the foundation of the world."
Matthew 25:34

*J*esus said that blessed ones feed the hungry, give water to the thirsty, welcome the stranger, clothe the naked, and visit the sick and imprisoned, never guessing that they serve Jesus Himself. Having read the Bible, I know, and have no excuses. Neither am I a saint, or a nun. As a daughter, sister, wife, mother, friend, and church member, I have done most of these things. Do I do them often enough? Only You know. What I have done I offer to You: with faith that when I do these things, I taste life in Your kingdom here and now; with hope that I have become a blessing; and with charity, remembering that "often, often, often, goes Christ in the stranger's guise."[11]

---

[11] from a Celtic rune. See http://celtic-spirituality.net/what-is-christian-celtic-spirituality/

April 29 — St. Catherine of Siena

*"It was love that made you create us and give us
being just so that we might taste your
supreme eternal good."*
—*Catherine of Siena* [12]

*"Blessed are you, Simon son of Jonah!
For flesh and blood has not revealed this to you,
but my Father in heaven."*
Matthew 16:17

Simon Peter's blessedness, like Mary's in the Visitation
(Lk 1:45), is the happiness that arises from being highly
favored with the revelation that Jesus is the Christ, Your
Son. [13] Their joy is a sign that the kingdom of heaven is
present within and among them. It is an intense joy that
far outweighs the costs of discipleship. In that moment,
time and space are united and the meaning of the cross is
realized: Jesus is recognized as the bridge between You and
humanity; Your will is done "on earth as it is in heaven." Will
there ever be such a moment on earth for me? Jesus, the
good shepherd, calls me by name to his table saying, "Do
this in remembrance of me." (Lk 22:19) The eucharist is my
foretaste of the heavenly banquet that is already but not yet;
sharing Your joy, I become a blessing.

---

[12] Ronda De Sola Chervin, *Prayers of the Women Mystics* (Ann Arbor, MI,
Servant Publications, 1992), p. 77.
[13] *See* n. 9.

April 30 — Sarah Josepha Buell Hale,
Editor and Prophetic Witness

"The great error of those who would sever the Union
rather than see a slave within its borders, is,
that they forget the master is their brother, as well as the
servant; and that the spirit which seeks to do good to all and
evil to none is the only true Christian philanthropy." [14]

"Blessed are your eyes, for they see, and your ears, for they hear."
Matthew 13:16

$\mathcal{B}$efore I get too complacent, Jesus' next sentence warns me: "Many prophets and holy people longed to see what you see, and never saw it; to hear what you hear, and never heard it." The human tendency is to see, but not perceive; hear, but not understand, in fear of being converted by You. In the weeks to come I will remember that Easter is not a point of arrival from which I can turn my attention to other things. The stories of Jesus' appearances after his death remind me that appearances can be deceiving. Am I willing to let what I see and hear enter not only my brain but my heart; to let sight become perception and hearing become understanding; and to be changed? Resurrection is not an event but the beginning of a process: a willingness to be vulnerable to what I see and hear, an openness to Your call to become a blessing.

---

[14] http://en.wikipedia.org/wiki/Sarah_Josepha_Buell_Hale

May:
the Season of Pentecost —
Receiving the Gifts of the
Holy Spirit

May 1

※

Suddenly they heard what sounded like a powerful wind
from heaven, the noise of which filled the entire house in
which they were sitting; and something appeared to them
that seemed like tongues of fire; these separated and
came to rest on the head of each of them.
They were all filled with the Holy Spirit.
Acts 2:2-4

When Jesus was baptized, the Holy Spirit descended on Him in the form of a dove. Why, at Pentecost, did the Holy Spirit descend on the disciples in the form of fire? The prophet Malachi asks, "Who can endure the day of his coming? For he is like a refiner's fire." (Mal 3:2) Jesus, already pure, needed no refining, but I do. The good news is that I, like the disciples, can endure the purifying fire of the Spirit and emerge from it a new creation, endowed with all the gifts of the Spirit: grace upon grace, strength upon strength, so that I may live in Your kingdom. This month, warmed and cheered by the glow of holy fire, I will explore the gifts of Pentecost.

May 2

Then afterward I will pour out my spirit on all flesh;
your sons and daughters shall prophesy,
old men shall dream dreams, your young men shall see visions.
Even on the male and female slaves, in those days,
I will pour out my spirit.
Joel 2:28-29

The prophet Joel shares the secrets that You want me to hear. The day of the Lord is coming. It could be a day of darkness and gloom, yet You, being Love, must love; You long to shower indiscriminately on me the blessings of Your Spirit, unlimited by human categories. The gifts of prophecy and visions bridge the limits of time and space. Overcoming the distance created by sin, Your Son, the Good Shepherd, finds and brings me back, never to be lost again. (Lk 15:4-7) Jesus poured out His life so that Your Spirit could be poured out on all humankind. He is the gate through which the gifts of Your Spirit flow freely upon me.

May 3

❧

I will give them one heart, and put a new spirit within them;
I will remove the heart of stone from their flesh and
give them a heart of flesh, so that they may follow
my statutes and keep my ordinances and obey them.
Then they shall be my people and I will be their God.
Ezekiel 11:19-20

You want nothing other than to pour upon me the gifts of Your Spirit, so what is keeping me from living the abundant life that Jesus offers? It seems strange to admit that the biggest barrier to Your Spirit is within me. I don't think of myself as being hardhearted, but I like to feel that I have some control over my life, that I can choose what to do and even what to feel. And You know how busy I am; sometimes I don't have time or energy for my relationship with You. Does that make me hardhearted? What would it feel like to have a heart of flesh and a new spirit, to follow You without reserve? Courage is a gift of your Spirit that frees my heart from its armor of fear so that I can love You and others wholeheartedly.

May 4 — St. Monicca, Mother of Augustine of Hippo

"We opened wide the mouth of our heart, thirsting for those supernal streams of thy fountain, "the fountain of life" which is with thee, that we might be sprinkled with its waters according to our capacity and might in some measure weigh the truth of so profound a mystery." [1]

For I will pour out water on the thirsty soil, streams on the dry ground. I will pour my spirit upon your descendants, and my blessing on your offspring.
Isaiah 44:3

St. Monicca, the mother of the theologian and mystic, St. Augustine, was a mystic in her own right. The faith that Augustine articulated, the faith that formed me, exists in large part because of her great love of You, her devotion to the Christian faith, and her tireless efforts to have Augustine become a Christian. Reading his description of their mutual mystical vision, it is impossible to discern who led whom to the heights of union with You. Their thirst for living water is itself a gift of the Spirit, "gushing up to eternal life" (Jn 4:14), which Monicca and Augustine drew together from Your well. (Is 12:3)

---

[1] Augustine: *Confessions,* Book IX, ch. 10, pp. 295-95, http://www.fordham.edu/halsall/basis/confessions-bod.asp

May 5

❧

Then Samuel took the horn of oil, and anointed him in the presence of his brothers; and the spirit of the Lord came mightily upon David from that day forward.
1 Samuel 16:13

"The oil of gladness" is a phrase which puzzles one who thinks of oil mainly as food or fuel. The psalmist prays, "You love righteousness and hate wickedness. Therefore God has anointed you with the oil of gladness beyond your companions." (Ps 45:7) Having promised to renounce evil and accept Christ, a newly-baptized Christian is anointed with the oil of salvation, as David and Christ were anointed. In my church, the bishop who consecrates the oil prays "that those who are sealed with it may share in the royal priesthood of Jesus Christ." [2] The Spirit's gifts include joy in the knowledge that I am marked as Christ's own forever.

---

[2] *The Book of Common Prayer* (1979), p. 307.

May 6

*The spirit of God has made me, and the breath
of the Almighty gives me life.
Job 33:4*

Life, both at its most fundamental and its most phenomenal, is a gift of the Spirit. You formed the first human of dust from the soil, but he did not become a living being until You blew into his nostrils the breath of life. (Gen 2:7) With Jesus' death and Resurrection, an entirely new kind of life came into the world: life to the full (Jn 10:10), life without end (Jn 11:26). It is to this life that the Good Shepherd calls me, one of full communion with Him and all creation, celebrated at the heavenly banquet that is eucharist.

May 7 — Harriet Starr Cannon, Religious

"[Dr. Muhlenberg] found a young probationary Sister, rocking, as he lay wrapped in a blanket within her arms, a little boy very ill with the loathsome disease. She was singing a hymn for him, and the poor child smiled as he looked up to her face, and forgot his pain and restlessness. [She was]'The very ideal of a Sister of Charity.' It was Sister Harriet." [3]

Here is my servant whom I uphold, my chosen, in whom my soul delights; the one upon whom I have put my spirit.
Isaiah 42:1

Sister Harriet, founder of the Sisters of Mercy, dedicated her life to caring for the least: the sick; children; and desperate, impoverished women. As she cradled the little boy ravaged by disease did she know that she was cradling You? As she sang to him did she feel Your delight? I like to think that their moment of bliss was a gift of Your Spirit; that, as they rocked, wrapped in Your strong, encircling arms, they felt Your kingdom come on earth as it is in heaven.

---

[3] http://anglicanhistory.org/bios/harriet, n. 2

May 8 — St. Julian of Norwich

*"In our good Lord the Holy Spirit we have our reward
and our gift for our living and our labour, endlessly surpassing
all that we desire in marvellous courtesy,
out of his great plentiful grace."*
—*Julian of Norwich* [4]

*Jesus said to them, "Peace be with you. As the Father
has sent me, so I send you." When he had said this,
breathed on them and said to them, "Receive the Holy Spirit."*
John 20:21-22

*I*t is evening. The disciples have heard from Mary of Magdala that she has seen the Lord; they are in hiding. Grief-stricken, fearful, bewildered, they wait. Suddenly Jesus is among them. Reassuring them, He says, "Peace be with you." Empowering them to carry on, He says, "As the Father sent me, so I am sending you." Is He reluctant to leave these dear friends? Like You did so many years ago with Adam, He breathes on them—such an intimate act! — so that they will be forever united with Him and with each other. Today, as then, the gift of the Holy Spirit dispels fear and penetrates barriers, releasing a force that can be resisted but not conquered, a force for peace and unity that empowers me to work for Your kingdom.

---

[4] *In Her Words; Women's Writings in the History of Christian Thought,* Amy Oden, ed., (Nashville, TN: Abingdon Press, 1994), p. 184.

May 9

*I will pour out a spirit of compassion and supplication
on the house of David and the inhabitants of Jerusalem,
so that, when they look on the one whom they have pierced,
they shall mourn for him, as one mourns for an only child.*
Zechariah 12:10

When someone looks like an enemy, compassion is the last thing on my mind; I want to protect myself. To some people in Jerusalem, Jesus looked like the enemy, a traitor to His own people. Jesus knew that He was caught in the trap of their mistaken fear, that He had to suffer and die to save the people who wanted Him dead, but He did not try to protect himself. Instead, as He hung on the cross He prayed for You to forgive them "for they know not what they do." (Lk 23:34) On Pentecost, the disciples were filled with the Holy Spirit and immediately began to preach to the Jews that the one they had handed over to be crucified was sent by You to save them. Hearing this, "they were cut to the heart" and asked to be baptized. (Acts 2:37-38) That moment of compassion and supplication was a gift of Your Spirit. When I am fearful and defensive, Your Spirit creates the bridge over which I return to You.

May 10

I am with you and my spirit remains among you.
Do not be afraid!
Haggai 2:4-5

*W*as Jesus thinking of these words of Haggai when, in the parable of the true vine, He used the word *remain* 10 times to reassure the disciples that He would always be with them? "Remain in me as I remain in You. . . I am the vine, you are the branches. Those who remain in me and I in them bear much fruit." (Jn 15:4-5) Although anticipating torture and death, Jesus said, "I have told you this so that my own joy may be in you and your joy be complete." (Jn 15:11) He knows that where You remain there can be no fear. (1 Jn 4:18) When I am tempted to fear, help me remember that You remain in me.

May 11

※

*The angel of the Lord appeared to Joseph in a dream
and said, "Joseph son of David, do not be afraid to
take Mary home as your wife, because she has conceived
what is in her by the Holy Spirit."*
Matthew 1:20

That Jesus is the greatest gift of the Holy Spirit is a truth so fundamental, mysterious, and vast, I need Your help to think about it. Out of the kaleidoscope of colors refracted by that Light, what do You want me to see today? There is the theme echoing down the millennia, heard in yesterday's reading from Haggai: do not be afraid. Mary's pregnancy gave Joseph strong reasons, both personal and social, to fear taking her as his wife, yet he obeyed Your instruction to marry her because he believed that the child in her womb came from Your Spirit. Had he followed his own inclination, what might the cost have been to Your kingdom? When I feel inspired to do Your will and fear the consequences, help me to trust the Spirit and follow through.

May 12

Teach me to do your will, for you are my God.
Let your good spirit lead me on a level path.
Psalm 143:10

"Prepare the way!" says Isaiah. "Let every valley be filled in, every mountain and hill be laid low, let every cliff become a plain, and the ridges a valley; then the glory of the Lord shall be revealed." What could Isaiah mean? How can I make a level path? Isaiah says You will lead me. (Is 40:3-11) Ezekiel speaks Your words of hope: "I am going to look after my flock myself and keep all of it in view. As a shepherd keeps all his flock in view when he stands up in the middle of his scattered sheep, so shall I keep my sheep in view. I shall rescue them from wherever they have been scattered." (Ezek 34:11-12) No obstacle, high or low, can block the shepherd's way. Maybe Isaiah's prophecy is not a command but an announcement: the Spirit is preparing a level path within me so that Your glory may be revealed.

May 13 — Frances Perkins, Public Servant and Prophetic Witness

"I came to Washington to serve God, FDR, and the poor working man."[5]
—Frances Perkins

The spirit of the Lord God is upon me, because the Lord has anointed me; he has sent me to bring good news to the oppressed.
Isaiah 61:1

When I look at the list of gifts of the Holy Spirit I think of how they will benefit me; but I am not alone, I am a branch on the true vine, a member of the body of Christ. (Jn 15) A vine does not exist apart from its branches; without the branches there is no vine; thus, whatever happens to one branch affects the entire vine. Frances Perkins used the gifts of the Spirit to bring justice and protection to the weakest branches on the vine. She took to heart Jesus' words, "Truly I tell you, just as you did it to one of the least of these who are members of my family, you did it to me." (Mt 25:40) At baptism, I was anointed and the Spirit came upon me, showering me with Your gifts. When I use those gifts, the whole vine becomes stronger.

---

[5] http://www.anglicanexaminer.com/Perkins-1.html

May 14

🙊

Being therefore exalted at the right hand of God, and
having received from the Father the promise of the Holy Spirit,
he has poured out this that you both see and hear.
Acts 2:33

You told Moses to construct a sanctuary so that You could dwell among Your people. (Ex 25:8) In spite of all You did before their eyes, and all that Moses said, Your people had no mind to understand, or eyes to see, or ears to hear. (Deut 29:4) Jesus said, "The kingdom of God is among you," yet its secrets were hidden within parables in order that "they may see and see again, but not perceive; may hear and hear again, but not understand." (Mk 4:11) Jesus' death and Resurrection reconciled humankind with You, making the gifts of the Spirit available to all. That Spirit was poured out on me at baptism that I might perceive Your kingdom here on earth. Do I look or avert my gaze? Do I listen or tune You out?

May 15

✻

*"Do not worry about how you are to speak or what
you are to say; for it is not you who speak, but the
Spirit of your Father speaking through you."
Matthew 10:19-20*

I enjoy reading the call of Moses. I imagine his initial shock
and terror changing to amazement and elation when You
say, "I have seen the miserable state of my people in Egypt.
I mean to deliver them out of the hands of the Egyptians."
Then he hears, "I send *you* to Pharaoh to bring my people
out of Egypt." (Ex 3:7-8, 10) Moses' protests are of no avail:
"What if they will not believe me or listen to my words?"
You answer, "I shall help you to speak and tell you what
to say." (Ex 4:10-12) When Jesus sends the disciples out,
He is candid about the dangers they will face from hostile
authorities. He doesn't say they will be safe; instead He says,
"Do not worry about what you will say." There is a cost to
discipleship. [6] The gift of the Holy Spirit is not safety, but
courage borne of faith that Your voice is speaking through
me.

---

[6] *The Cost of Discipleship, See* March 7, n.3.

May 16 — The Martyrs of Sudan

Look upon us, O Creator who has made us.
God of all peoples, we are yearning for our land.
Hear the prayer of our souls in the wilderness.
Hear the prayer of our bones in the wilderness.
Hear our prayer as we call out to you.[7]

The Lord God said to me, "Prophesy to these bones,
and say to them, O dry bones, hear the word of the Lord.
Thus says the Lord God to these bones: I will cause
breath to enter you and you shall live."
Ezekiel 37:4-5

*A*re these the bones of martyrs or of their murderers? Who is more dead: those whose faith cost them their lives, or the soulless ones who killed them? The Spirit can never die, no matter that it lives in people that are killed. Like Able's, their blood cries out to You. (Gen 4:10) When Jesus came to see Martha and Mary after Lazarus died, they said to Him, "If you had been here, my brother would not have died." Jesus, moved to tears, called Lazarus out of his tomb. You are the Christ, the Son of God; anyone who believes in You, even though he or she dies, will live. (Jn 11:21-44) What about those who don't believe, who kill those who do? Can You breathe life into their bones? Can You call their dead souls to life?

---

[7]*Holy Women, Holy Men*, p. 370.

May 17

❦

A shoot shall come out from the stump of Jesse, and a
branch shall grow out of his roots. The spirit of the Lord
shall rest on him,
Isaiah 11:1-2

*I*t is interesting for a change to imagine Your Spirit at rest. The Spirit that hovered over the waters at creation, that animated Adam and the dry bones; that Spirit is Your messenger, restlessly seeking faithful ones to do Your will. In Mary, the restless Spirit finds the perfect vessel within which to gestate the perfection of humanity, Jesus. No longer seeking, the Spirit rests hidden in the womb, awaiting the birth of the One who will prepare all human hearts to receive its gifts. But the Spirit's work isn't done. On Jesus Your Spirit rests; in Him, Your kingdom is already but not yet. From Pentecost to today and into the future, the Spirit continues to seek a home in every human heart until all humanity is united in You. Holy Spirit, come! Rest in me.

May 18

the spirit of wisdom,
Isaiah 11:2

*J*ames' letter warns of the danger of speech: "no one can tame the tongue. With it we bless the Lord, and curse those who are made in the likeness of God." (Jas 3:8-9) I am generally a thoughtful person, not impulsive, self-aware, and yet You know there is more than one kind of spirit in my heart, and my speech can be motivated by any of them. How can I use the Spirit's gift of wisdom? James describes two kinds of wisdom: one is boastful and false to the truth; the other peaceable, gentle, willing to yield, full of mercy, without partiality or hypocrisy. One is earthly, unspiritual, devilish; the other is "from above." I am wise when I stop before I speak to examine my heart: what am I trying to accomplish? Who, besides me, will be served by what I say? What is the goal? James says, "A harvest of righteousness is sown in peace for those who make peace." (Jas 3:18)

May 19

🎔

the spirit of understanding,
Isaiah 11:2

𝒫aul speaks of those who are "darkened in their understanding, alienated from the life of God because of their ignorance and hardness of heart." (Eph 4:18) His description is graphic: they walk in the futility of their minds. I picture a bleak, Kafkaesque existence, senseless, disorienting, and pointless.[8] Thanks to the Spirit's gift of understanding I am not alienated; instead I am as a sheep to her shepherd, as a branch to a vine. I am not disoriented; instead, like a flower toward the sun, I turn always toward You. My life is not futile; instead I collaborate toward Your goal of full communion of all creation with You. When life seems menacing, I need not worry, but only pray to You with thanksgiving, and Your peace, which surpasses all understanding, will guard my heart and mind in Christ. (Phil 4:6-7)

---

[8]http://en.wiktionary.org/wiki/Kafkaesque

May 20

the spirit of counsel
Isaiah 11:2

*I*n the time before Christ, before Abraham, people worshipped gods and goddesses who acted capriciously. Human life was seen as "a pale reenactment of the life of the eternal heavens, ruled by a fate beyond the pitifully limited powers of human beings. The gods decided." Their will might be divined by those with secret priestly knowledge, but one's fate was written in the stars and could not be changed. [9] Where would I be without Your gift of counsel? It is too awful to contemplate. Your counsel has given me strength and given my life direction; knowing I can rely on it has replaced despair with hope and peace. How can I make a return to You for all the good You have done for me? May I live each day in grateful obedience to Your loving counsel.

---

[9] Thomas Cahill, *The Gifts of the Jews; How a Tribe of Desert Nomads Changed the Way Everyone Thinks and Feels,* (New York: Anchor Books, 1998), p. 46.

May 21

✿

the spirit of might,
Isaiah 11:2

*I*n the movie, *Chariots of Fire*, the missionary, Eric Liddell, uses his talent as a runner to testify to Your glory. Bound to Paris to compete in the Olympics, Liddell learns that his race will take place on a Sunday. Although under intense national pressure, he refuses to run because his religious convictions prohibit running on the Sabbath. That Sunday, Liddell delivers a sermon based on Isaiah 40: "But they that wait upon the Lord shall renew their strength; they shall mount up with wings as eagles, they shall run and not be weary." One of Liddell's teammates offers him his place in a much longer race; though not favored to win, Liddell gains the gold medal. He compares faith to running in a race: "It's hard. It requires concentration of will, energy of soul. . . And where does the power come from to see the race to its end? From within." That power is a gift of the Holy Spirit.

May 22

🜨

the spirit of knowledge,
Isaiah 11:2

*K*nowledge, as Adam and Eve discovered, is not a thing to be taken like fruit from a tree; it is obtained only as a gift from You. When Solomon succeeded his father, David, as king, he approached Your altar humbly. When You invited him to ask for a gift, Solomon asked for wisdom and knowledge to govern the people. You answered, "Since you have asked not for riches, honor, or a long life, but for wisdom and knowledge, therefore wisdom and knowledge are granted you, and also treasure and honor such as none other has had or will ever have." (2 Chr 1:5-12) Before his death and Resurrection, Jesus said, "The Advocate, the Holy Spirit, whom the Father will send in my name, will teach you everything." (Jn 14:26) This precious gift of knowledge is mine to hold, to guard, and to treasure, with the help of the Holy Spirit living in me. (2 Tim 1:13-14)

May 23

the spirit of fear of the Lord.
The fear of the Lord is his breath.
Isaiah 11:2

Jewish tradition teaches that fear of the Lord is conscience, beginning as an unreflective fear of consequences, and maturing into an awareness of what You want and do. It is the knowledge that keeps me from doing evil, even when no one is watching. [10] Isaiah says that conscience is the breath, or spirit, of the Messiah. When You created Adam, You breathed into his nostrils. (Gen 2:7) When Jesus appeared to the disciples after his Resurrection, He breathed on them and said, "Receive the Holy Spirit." (Jn 20:22) Conscience, the gift You give so intimately, is my very life breath, enabling me to walk in Your ways, to love You and serve You with all my heart and soul. (Deut 10:12)

---

[10] *The Jewish Study Bible,* p. 1450, n. 7.

May 24

"The wind blows where it chooses, and you hear the
sound of it, but you do not know where it comes from
or where it goes. So it is with everyone who is
born of the Spirit."
John 3:8

The gifts of the Spirit are, like any new life, palpable and unpredictable. When a baby is born, the parents wonder, "Who is this child?" So it is with anyone who receives the gifts of the Holy Spirit, no matter her years. Paul says, "if anyone is in Christ, there is a new creation: everything old has passed away; see, everything has become new!" (2 Cor 5:17) It sounds exciting, and disturbing. At baptism I received the Holy Spirit. I used to think of this as something ceremonial, like an honorary degree from a university, mainly for show. What if Paul's words are as true for me as they were for the early Christians? What if, all through my life, Your Spirit has been creating me anew? What might I have been without Your Spirit? What might I become?

May 25

✤

While Jesus after his own baptism was at prayer,
heaven opened and the Holy Spirit descended on him in
bodily shape, like a dove. And a voice came from heaven,
"You are my Son, the Beloved; my favor rests on you."
Luke 3:21-22

At the baptism of Jesus, God incarnate, Your Spirit descended incarnate in the form of a dove, a sign that You came among us in an entirely new way. To make Your purposes clear, You sent Your Spirit upon Jesus in the ancient symbol of peace. Beautiful upon the mountain are the feet of the Prince of Peace who announces salvation. (Is 52:7) The acceptable time, the day of salvation, is here and now. At Pentecost, You sent Your Spirit to be incarnated forever in the Body of Christ, of which I am a member. Holy Spirit, rest Your favor on me. Make me an instrument of Your peace.

May 26

﷽

And the Spirit immediately drove him out
into the wilderness.
Mark 1:12

*I*mmediately after his baptism, the Holy Spirit drove Jesus into the wilderness to be tempted by Satan. Mark depicts Jesus in the grip of a great force, recalling Jacob wrestling with the stranger—an angel? You?—at the river before crossing into the promised land. The wilderness, the place of encounter with You, is also the place of blessing. Jacob did not let the stranger go until he gave Jacob a blessing and a new name, "Israel, for you have striven with God and with humans, and have prevailed." (Gen 32:26-29) When there is turmoil in my life, could it be the Spirit driving me to wrestle with my inner demons, in those unexplored places in my heart where, like Jacob, I fear to tread? The courage to stay and wrestle is a gift of the Spirit; the blessing is in the struggle.

May 27 — Saint Bertha of Kent

*Bertha became the wife of Ethelbert, king of Kent, on condition
that she be allowed to remain a Christian and be attended by
a bishop. It was partly due to her influence that Ethelbert was
induced to receive Augustine and to be baptized.
Pope Gregory, in 601, addressed a letter to Bertha, in which he
compliments her highly on her faith and knowledge of letters, and
urges her to make still greater efforts for the spread of Christianity.
He also ascribes the conversion of the English mainly to her.* [11]

*I have called him by name and filled him with
divine spirit, with ability, intelligence, and knowledge,
so that they may make all that I have commanded you.
Exodus 31:1-3, 6*

When You wanted a place in the desert where You might dwell among Your people, You called Betzalel, a former slave, by name and filled him with Your spirit so that he would know how to create the ornate and gorgeous Tent of Meeting. (Ex 31:1-5) When You wanted a place in England to dwell, You called Bertha, Queen of Kent, by name to foster the introduction of Christianity to England, filling her with Your divine spirit and the ability to restore an ancient church in Canterbury. Thanks to Bertha, St. Augustine was received there in 596 to preach the Gospel. The Holy Spirit uses our limited human capacities to create the instruments through which Your kingdom can grow and spread. In awe and gratitude, I pray, "My soul magnifies the Lord, and my spirit rejoices in God my savior." (Lk 1:46)

---

[11] http://www.ccel.org/ccel/wace/biodict.html?term=Bertha,%20wife%20of%20
Ethelbert,%20king%20of%20Kent

May 28

Now raised to the heights by God's right hand,
Jesus has received from the Father the Holy Spirit,
who was promised, and what you see and hear is
the outpouring of that Spirit.
Acts 2:33

Of the coming of the Messiah, Isaiah says, "On that day the deaf shall hear the words of a scroll, and out of their gloom and darkness the eyes of the blind shall see." (Is 29:18) Not long before his death and Resurrection, Jesus spoke of the prophets and righteous people who longed to see and hear but did not. (Mt 13:17) He asked the disciples, "Do you have eyes, and fail to see? Do you have ears, and fail to hear?" (Mk 8:18) At Pentecost *that day* prophesied by Isaiah became today: eyes were unveiled and ears unstopped by the outpouring of the Spirit, for all and forever more. Standing with the crowd, I hear Peter's words as if for the first time and receive anew the outpouring of the Spirit's gifts. Isaiah speaks Your challenge to me, "You have heard; now see all this; will you not declare it?" (Is 48:6)

May 29

✻

May the God of hope fill you with all joy and
peace in believing, so that you may
abound in hope by the power of the Holy Spirit.
Romans 15:13

A certain kind of hope, the hope that persists in the face of overwhelming evidence to the contrary, is a gift of the Holy Spirit. Paul speaks of the hope of Abraham who, at age 100, was beyond hope, and nevertheless believed that he would become a father of many nations. (Rom 4:18-19) Paul boasted of his hope that he would share Your glory, knowing that he could be killed at any moment. His abundance of hope enabled him to boast even of his sufferings, because, through the gift of Your love "poured into our hearts through the Holy Spirit," he knew that "suffering produces endurance, and endurance produces character, and character produces hope, and hope does not disappoint us." (Rom 5:2-5) When circumstances seem bleak, help me remember that all the hope I need to persevere is already mine, a gift of Your Spirit.

May 30 — St. Joan of Arc,
Mystic and Soldier

*[I]f she were in a wood, that is in a quiet place, she
could hear the voices coming towards her. She added . . . that it
seemed to her a noble voice, and that she believed it came from
God; the voice always came quite clearly to her,
and she understood it well.* [12]

*A voice said, "Stand up; I am going to speak to you."
As he said these words the spirit came into me and
made me stand up, and I heard him speaking to me.
He said, "Son of man, I am sending you."
Ezekiel 2:1-3*

The ability to stand up for You is a gift of the Holy Spirit.
The suffering servant says: "The Lord God helps me;
therefore I know that I shall not be put to shame; he who
vindicates me is near. Who will contend with me? Let us
stand up together." (Is 50:7-8) At age 12, Joan saw visions of
Sts. Michael, Catherine, and Margaret, who told her to drive
out the English from France. At age 16, she traveled through
hostile territory in male disguise to advise the king on tactics.
She rode at the head of the army, wearing the equipment
of a knight, and led a series of victories that reversed the
tide of the war. Captured by the English, she was tried for
heresy and executed by burning. During her trial, when she
was asked if she knew she was in God's grace, she answered,
"If I am not, may God put me there; and if I am, may God
so keep me." [13]

---

[12]http://www.authorama.com/jeanne-d-arc-14.html
[13]http://en.wikipedia.org/wiki/St._Joan_of_Arc

May 31—The Visitation of the
Blessed Virgin Mary

When Elizabeth heard Mary's greeting, the child leaped
in her womb. And Elizabeth was filled with the Holy Spirit.
Luke 1:41

The Spirit is Your breath; it speaks through Your chosen ones with power. Hearing the angel's announcement that she will bear the Messiah, Mary is filled with the Spirit and Jesus begins to grow within her. Hearing Mary's greeting, Elizabeth is filled with the Spirit and proclaims in a loud voice the Messiah's presence within Mary. When Elizabeth and Zechariah go to the temple to circumcise John, the Spirit opens Zechariah's mouth and all hear him prophesy the birth of the Messiah. (Lk 1:67-78) Voice after voice, the circle of those who hear widens until Pentecost when the disciples, filled with the Holy Spirit, are heard by everyone in their own language. (Acts 2:4) The circle continues to expand, for there are other sheep, not of this fold, whom the Shepherd must bring. Through the Holy Spirit they will hear his voice, and in that moment of hearing, there will be one flock and one Shepherd.

June:
Growing Time

June 1

🦋

The Lord God planted a garden in
Eden/Land-of-Pleasure, in the east,
and there he placed the human whom he had formed.
Genesis 2:8

𝒴ou who are all-powerful, all-sufficient; You who are the source of all love, nevertheless want — need? — relationship. You created Adam and Eve and put them in Eden, the land of pleasure, together with everything they needed to grow with You in love. In the church year the time between Pentecost and Advent is called ordinary time; not ordinary in the usual, mundane sense, but all the time outside of the seasons of Lent and Easter, Advent and Christmas. The liturgical color for ordinary time is green, the color for growing. This month, and all through ordinary time, I will dwell with You in the land of pleasure, growing in love.

June 2 — St. Blandina and Her Companions, the Martyrs of Lyons

"I am a Christian, and we commit no wrongdoing." [1]
— *St. Blandina*

*The righteous flourish like the palm tree, and grow
like a cedar in Lebanon.*
Psalm 92:12

*B*landina was a slave, tortured because she would not renounce Christ and worship the state gods of Rome. What does that have to do with me, nearly two millennia later in a more enlightened place and age? We have no established religion nor state gods—or do we? How do I feel about people who worship You, though not Christ? When I make decisions do I consult You or rely on other gods? Am I willing to follow Your commandments and accept the consequences, or do I lie low and tell myself it doesn't matter? Although a woman and a slave, Blandina knew that in Christ she was Your daughter, equal to all. (Gal 3:28) Somehow that made her strong enough to face her torturers unafraid. Could I take courage from her example and grow?

---

[1] http://en.wikipedia.org/wiki/Blandina

June 3

꩜

The Lord God caused to spring up from the soil every
type of tree, desirable to look at and good to eat,
and the Tree of Life in the midst of the garden
and the Tree of the Knowing
of Good and Evil.
Genesis 2:9

*W*hy, if You didn't want Adam and Eve to eat of it, did you plant the Tree of the Knowing of Good and Evil in the midst of the garden? Any parent could tell you that was a disaster waiting to happen. The Easter vigil liturgy gives thanks for their sin:

> O happy fault,
> O necessary sin of Adam,
> which gained for us so great a Redeemer! [2]

St. Augustine said that You thought it better to bring good out of evil than to allow no evil to exist. [3] Could the evil in my life be a gift given so that, through Christ, I can grow stronger in my relationship with You?

---

[2] http://en.wikipedia.org/wiki/Exsultet#Roman_Catholic_English_and_Latin_Text
[3] http://en.wikipedia.org/wiki/Felix_culpa

June 4

Now a river goes out from Eden, to water the garden,
and from there it divides and becomes four stream-heads.
Genesis 2:10

*N*o garden can flourish without water. From Christ, the living water, flow four streams, the four gospels; together with the sacraments they water the garden that is Your church. In Jesus' time, during the Feast of Booths, Jews recalled Ezekiel's vision of streams flowing from the temple and prayed for life-giving water. (Ez 47:1) On the seventh day of the festival worshippers processed around the temple chanting prayers for the return of the Messiah.[4] Jesus confided to the woman at the well, "If you knew the gift of God, and who it is that is saying to you, 'Give me a drink,' you would have asked him and he would have given you living water." (Jn 4:10) Now, on this, the greatest day of the festival, Jesus stands and cries out, "Let anyone who is thirsty come to me, and let the one who believes in me drink!" (Jn 7:37-38) I come, leaving my water jar behind.

---

[4] http://en.wikipedia.org/wiki/Hoshana_Rabbah#Prayers_for_Messiah

June 5

🎕

The Lord God took the human and set him in the garden of
Eden, to work it and to watch it.
Genesis 2:15

*Y*ou planted a garden for us (Gen 2:8); how readily we focus instead on the Fall. (Gen 3) How much has been written and said about the Fall, and how little has been told of that garden? What is it about a garden that makes it the place of Your choosing? In *The Secret Garden*,[5] Mary, a spoiled 10-year-old orphan, is sent to live in England with her uncle, a widower. Confined to two rooms and told to amuse herself, she hears mysterious crying at night. A servant tells her of a private garden tended by her late aunt; after her death, her uncle locked the garden and buried the key. With the help of a robin (there's the Spirit again!), Mary finds the key and begins to tend the garden, which brings healing to her and the whole household. Could the garden be a place of healing for me? This month I will visit or tend one and discover its secrets for myself.

---

[5] Frances Hodgson Burnett, *The Secret Garden* (New York, Penguin Books, 1987).

June 6

✠

*If you will only heed his every commandment—loving the
Lord your God, and serving him with all your heart and with
all your soul then he will give the rain for your land in its
season, and you will gather in your grain, your wine, and your
oil; and you will eat your fill.*
Deuteronomy 11:13-15

When Jesus was tempted to command stones to become
loaves of bread He answered, "One does not live by bread
alone, but by every word that comes from the mouth of
God." (Mt 4:3-4) Your word is nourishment. When I love
you and live in accord with Your will my life becomes a fertile
garden. On a page, Your word, like seed, can seem lifeless,
yet when planted in me and watered with living water, Your
word springs up like waves of golden grain, "miracle upon
miracle, nothing less than resurrection from the dead."[6] It
yields a harvest for the heavenly banquet of rich food and of
fine wines, "which earth has given and human hands have
made,"[7] the bread of life and cup of salvation at eucharist.

---

[6] Joachim Jeremias, *The Parables of Jesus* (Upper Saddle River, NJ, Prentice Hall, 1972), p. 149.
[7] http://catholic-resources.org/ChurchDocs/Mass.htm#Eucharist

June 7

※

For the Lord will comfort Zion; he will comfort
all her waste places, and will make her wilderness like Eden,
her desert like the garden of the Lord; joy and gladness will
be found in her, thanksgiving and the voice of song.
Isaiah 51:3

In the sunny, breezy days of June, it is easy to avert my eyes from the waste places within me. All around are green growing things, trees in full leaf and flowers in bloom. The glorious gifts of Easter and Pentecost sit as if on a shelf in my heart, yet You, the eager giver of these gifts, are impatient for me to open them. You, who planted a garden, cannot rest until my inner desert is irrigated with the water of life. You cannot wait to see my heart burst into flowers of joy and gladness, thanksgiving and song, an Eden in which I may find You walking in the cool of the day.

June 8

If you offer your food to the hungry and satisfy the needs
of the afflicted, the Lord will guide you continually,
and satisfy your needs in parched places;
and you shall be like a watered garden, like a spring of water,
whose waters never fail.
Isaiah 58:10-11

When the dry days of summer stretch into weeks, it is obvious that water makes the difference between life and death: the plants brown, wither, and go dormant or die unless they are watered. On their way through the desert to the promised land, away from the daily presence of the Nile, the Hebrews slowly and painfully became aware of their complete dependence on You for water. As they entered the promised land You promised that if they followed your commandments and loved You completely, You would provide the rain—and the justice—they needed. (Deut 11:14-15) Jesus said, "Blessed are those who hunger and thirst for righteousness, for they will be filled." (Mt 5:6) Jesus' thirst for righteousness led Him to the cross, so that "justice would roll down like waters, and righteousness like an ever-flowing stream." (Am 5:24) I am a branch on the vine that is Christ. May his justice and righteousness flow through me.

June 9

*For as the earth brings forth its shoots, and as a
garden causes what is sown in it to spring up,
so the Lord God will cause righteousness and
praise to spring up before all the nations.*
Isaiah 61:11

*F*ive times Isaiah says that Your saving deeds *spring up,*
as plants seem to spring up from seed sown in the earth.
Curiously, he does not use the word *grow,* which is usually
associated with a garden. The implication is that Your
deeds—faithfulness, offspring, salvation, healing—appear
suddenly, without warning, we know not how. (Is 44:4, 45:8, 58:8)
Jesus sprang up out of the earth. The True Vine, the faithful
offspring whose death and resurrection brought salvation
and healing to the whole earth, sprang up from a tomb in a
garden. Heaven and earth embraced to create Him in whom
the words of the psalmist are realized: "Steadfast love and
faithfulness will meet; righteousness and peace will kiss
each other. Faithfulness will spring up from the ground, and
righteousness will look down from the sky." (Ps 85:10-11)

June 10

They shall come and sing aloud on the height of Zion,
and they shall be radiant over the goodness of the Lord,
over the grain, the wine, and the oil, and over the
young of the flock and the herd; their life shall
become like a watered garden, and they shall
never languish again.
Jeremiah 31:12

Jeremiah describes nothing less than a return to Eden, before the Fall, before Adam and Eve hid from You. No longer afraid, Your people come to the heights and sing aloud for joy. The soil, no longer accursed, bears grain, grape, and olive. The harvest is gathered and young are born without suffering. In the garden You planted, life is restored and watered eternally by living water, the resurrected life of Christ. Once again Your people walk with You in the cool of the day, now hand in hand, never to languish again.

June 11

🕮

A garden locked is my sister, my bride,
a garden locked, a fountain sealed.
Song of Solomon 4:12

*W*e lock things to protect what is inside from what is outside. When You, the insistent bridegroom, call, do I hide behind a locked door? (Lk 11:7) Who or what am I protecting? When Mary Magdalene ran from the garden where she met the risen Christ and announced to the disciples, "I have seen the Lord," they hid in fear behind a locked door. Then Jesus came and stood among them saying, "receive the Holy Spirit." (Jn 20:18-22) Jesus' death and resurrection is the key that unlocks the garden; the Spirit is the fountain unsealed. "The Spirit and the bride say, 'Come.' And let everyone who hears say, 'Come.' And let everyone who is thirsty come. Let anyone who wishes take the water of life as a gift." (Rev 22:17)

June 12

Fountain that makes the gardens fertile,
well of living water, streams flowing down from Lebanon.
Song of Solomon 4:15

These words are part of a poem of intense longing. Dreaming of his bride, thirsting for her presence, the writer pictures her as the source of unending love. The psalmist prays: "God, you are my God, I am seeking you, my soul is thirsting for you, my flesh is longing for you, a land parched, weary and waterless; I long to gaze on you in the Sanctuary, and to see your power and glory. Your love is better than life itself." (Ps 63:1-3) I have prayed this prayer to You, yet You are the bridegroom and we, your people, are the bride. (Rev 21:9-10) Maybe I have missed the point. Maybe the poetic words of the Song are not about me wanting You, but about You wanting me.

June 13

Awake, north wind, come, wind of the south!
Breathe over my garden, to spread its sweet smell around.
Song of Solomon 4:16

*I*n the beginning, a wind swept over the earth creating new life. (Gen 1:2) After the Flood, when the waters receded, a wind blew over the earth bringing new life to all creation; the earth, no longer cursed, became Your garden once again. (Gen 7-8) When You brought Your people out of Egypt You drove the sea back with a strong wind so that they could cross on dry land out of slavery and into freedom. (Ex 14:21) At Pentecost, as wind filled the house where the disciples were, they became a new creation, freed from fear and eager to do Your will. (Acts 2:2) Come, Holy Spirit, breathe on me! Create me anew!

June 14

Let my Beloved come into his garden,
let him taste its rarest fruits.
Song of Solomon 4:16

*D*esire is the fruit at the heart of Your garden. No sooner had You separated light from dark, and waters from earth, than You created fruit, as if You long had it in mind as a particular treat to share with Your future companions. (Gen 1-2) The rarest fruit is in the middle (of the garden? of life?), the fruit of knowing good from evil. Eve, seeing that fruit was to be desired, took, ate, and shared it with Adam. Innocence and paradise were lost, but gained was the rarest fruit of all. Through the death and resurrection of Jesus, Key of David, the gates of Your garden were thrown open. No longer a locked garden, Your people are free to love You. No longer forbidden, Your knowledge fills the earth as the waters cover the sea. (Is 11:9)

June 15

✣

*"My whole religious life and experience seem centered with
increasing vividness on our Lord. Sometimes the sense of
His Presence is so vivid, I wonder what will happen next."* [8]
—Evelyn Underhill

*I come to my garden, my sister, my bride;
I gather my myrrh with my spice, I eat my honeycomb
with my honey, I drink my wine with my milk. Eat, friends,
drink, and be drunk with love.*
Song of Solomon 5:1

Can a woman with a so-called normal life love You with all
her heart, soul, and mind? Although fully engaged in life as
an author, educator, and wife in Edwardian England, Evelyn
Underhill's relationship with You was intense and intimate,
including daily writing, research, prayer, and meditation.
Understanding that incarnation, God-with-us, means that
holiness is no longer limited to a certain time, place, or kind
of life, Underhill walked with You in the garden, tasting its
rarest fruits in her mystical experiences. For her, as for the
bride in the Song of Solomon, the winter was past. Life: new,
unquenchable, and lovely, came to meet her with the dawn. [9]

---

[8] Steven Fanning, *Mystics of the Christian Tradition* (New York, Routledge,
2006), p. 211.
[9] Margaret Cropper, *The Life of Evelyn Underhill* (New York, Harper and
Brothers, 1958) p. 47. *See http://en.wikipedia.org/wiki/Evelyn_Underhill*

June 16

And they will say, "This land that was desolate
has become like the garden of Eden; and the waste and desolate
and ruined towns are now inhabited and fortified."
Ezekiel 36:35

Using the word *desolate* five times in three verses, Ezekiel describes a kind of hell, yet he also paints a picture of startling change: the desolated land becomes not merely fruitful, but as abundant as the garden of Eden. The towns are not merely inhabited, but fortified against evil. What is going on? Exiled from their land, and, as they thought, from Your very presence, the Israelites suffered a kind of psychological death: "By the rivers of Babylon we sat and wept at the memory of Zion. How could we sing the Lord's song in a foreign land?" (Ps 137:1-4) Sometimes I feel like that: a stranger surrounded by strangers in a foreign land, unable to sing Your song, searching for Eden. Nevertheless, You enjoin me to love the stranger because, after all, the stranger is I. (Deut 10:19) You have gathered me, as You promised, into Your garden. If only I would open my eyes and see; open my ears and hear, and open my heart to embrace the stranger at my side, I would know it to be true.

June 17

🙎

I will be like the dew to Israel; he shall strike root
like the forests of Lebanon. His shoots shall spread out;
his beauty shall be like the olive tree. They shall again
live beneath my shadow, they shall flourish as a garden;
they shall blossom like the vine, their fragrance shall be like the
wine of Lebanon.
Hosea 14:5-7

*A*s if in time-lapse photography, Hosea describes a reversal of the effects of the Fall: previously cursed ground that bore only thorns and thistles revives under the refreshing dew of Your forgiveness. Trees take root and bear fruit not forbidden. The flourishing garden is protected by Your shade. Blossoms appear on the vine, harbingers of a loving union that will bear much fruit. (Jn 15) "Who is this arising like the dawn, fair as the moon, resplendent as the sun, terrible as an army with banners?" (Song 6:10) He is Christ, the bridegroom, coming to make all things new. (Rev 21:2-3)

June 18

Along the river will grow every kind of fruit tree
with leaves that never wither and fruit that never fails;
they will bear new fruit every month, because this
water comes from the sanctuary. And their fruit
will be good to eat and the leaves medicinal.
Ezekiel 47:12

The Israelites left Pharoah in Egypt where the river was a source of suffering and death, to follow You, who provided them the water of life in the desert. In Moab the king feared their numbers and asked his prophet, Balaam, to curse them. Instead, You sent Your Spirit upon Balaam, who declared to the king that Israel's camp was, "Like gardens by the banks of a river, like aloes planted by the Lord, like cedars beside the waters!" (Num 24:6) Those healing, life-giving waters that flowed from Your presence among the Hebrews are the same waters that covered the earth at creation and that watered the trees of Eden. They gave birth to Jesus, flowed over him at baptism, and out of his side as He, the source of living water, hung on the cross. These waters continue to nourish the grain and the grape, the good fruit that is eucharist; and now me as I take, eat, and drink the body and blood of Christ.

June 19

✣

*"Consider the lilies, how they grow: they neither toil
nor spin; yet I tell you, even Solomon in all his glory
was not clothed like one of these."*
Luke 12:27

Telling the disciples not to worry about what to wear, Jesus
says to consider the lilies. There are lilies on my table this
week, and truly, they are exquisite: their color the ivory of
old piano keys, their golden interiors flecked with dark
red, petals curving, the flowers nod on their stems with a
grace unmatched by any prima ballerina. Each time I look
at them I am astonished. Their intoxicating scent: sweet,
musky, and citrusy, fills the room like incense. How You
must love the beauty that You lavish on every created thing,
in incomprehensible variety! Being Love, perhaps beauty is
simply of the essence of You. Help me discover the particular
beauty You have created in me.

June 20

*"The kingdom of God is like a mustard seed that
someone took and sowed in the garden."*
Luke 13:19

I've thought a lot about the seed that Your kingdom is
like; today I am wondering why it was sowed in a garden.
I have a picture of a mustard tree in Israel and it is a very
ordinary, if large, shrub. It wouldn't be grown for its looks
or for its infinitesimal seeds, which are much tinier than the
seeds used to make mustard. What is it doing in a garden in
Your kingdom? Maybe the mustard tree has a beauty not
apparent in itself, but in the way it shelters all the birds of the
air in its branches, filling the garden with song. You do not
see as humans see; we look on outward appearances, but You
look on the heart. (1 Sam 16:7) Perhaps I have something
to learn about beauty from the mustard tree as well as from
the lily.

June 21

"I am the true vine, and my Father is the vinegrower."
John 15:1

Your garden includes a particular vine: Jesus, the True Vine. You, the vinegrower, prune the vine so that those clusters that remain will have the most concentrated sweetness, and thus will become the finest wine. Perhaps Jesus was thinking of his own life, soon to be cut short, when He said that every branch that bears fruit You prune to make it bear more fruit. At the Last Supper Jesus looked forward to the moment when He, the first and finest of fruits, would be pruned in order to become an entirely new kind of wine. He gave the disciples a cup saying, "this is my blood of the covenant, which is poured out for many." (Mk 14:24) The wine of eucharist, like sap, carries the risen life of Christ throughout its branches, a weekly infusion of grace that keep me on the Vine.

June 22

"Every branch that bears fruit he prunes that it may
bear much fruit."
John 15:2

As a gardener, I've learned that most plants grow better when they are pruned. Petunias need to be dead-headed in order to keep flowering. Tomato plants need to have the suckers trimmed off to produce well. When I prune my bushes they grow back the following spring fuller and more vibrant than before. I even imagine that they look happier. Why is it that pruning in my own life feels so awful? I'm told that when a mature grape vine is pruned the sap runs out like tears. Praying in the garden on the night of his arrest, Jesus' sweat poured out as drops of blood upon the ground. Perhaps it was his prayer to You that enabled Him to go on: "Father, if you are willing, remove this cup from me; yet, not my will but yours be done." (Lk 22:42-44) I may not welcome being pruned, but I might endure it more gracefully praying Jesus' prayer.

June 23

"Already you are pruned because of the word which I have spoken to you."
John 15:3

Pruning is a cutting away of dead or overgrown branches to increase fruitfulness and growth. How did Jesus' word prune the disciples so that they could grow and bear more fruit? "You have heard it said, 'You shall not murder'; but I say to you that if you are angry with a brother or sister, you will be liable to judgment. . . You have heard it said, 'You shall not swear falsely'; but I say to you, Do not swear at all, either by heaven or by the earth." Jesus pruned away the limits of the law to reveal Your limitless law of love: "You have heard it said, 'You shall love your neighbor and hate your enemy,' but I say to you, Love your enemies and pray for those who persecute you." (Mt 5:43-44) You must think very highly of me to ask such hard things. Help me grow into the person You created me to be.

June 24

✖

*"As the branch is not able to bear fruit unless it
remains on the vine, so neither can you unless
you remain in me."*
John 15:4

"*A*re we there yet?" Like a child on vacation, I anxiously wonder, "Am I there yet?" If my destination is You, the answer is yes. To be with You I don't need to go anywhere. What a relief that is! Day after day I rush, never realizing how anxious I am until, one day, I read that word *remain*. I exhale and feel my shoulders relax. Am I laboring for that which does not satisfy? Spending my money for that which is not bread? (Is 55:2) Have I forgotten that I already have the one thing that I need? Let me be like the sower, who, having scattered seed on the ground, sleeps peacefully in You. (Mk 4:26-27)

June 25

"I am the vine; you are the branches."
John 15:5

*W*e sat on the floor in a circle around the vine, several 6-
to 8-year-old children and I, our Bibles open to the parable
of the True Vine. Ours was an ordinary houseplant, a type
ubiquitous in homes and grade school classrooms. We took
turns, each reading one verse of the parable. At the end I
asked, "Can we tell where the vine ends and the branches
begin? If we cut off all the branches, would we still have a
vine?" The children shook their heads. On the night He told
them this parable, Jesus might have wanted reassurance as
much as his bewildered disciples. Perhaps He, too, needed
to remember how close they were to Him: even closer than
sheep to their shepherd, of the very fiber of his being. Today,
He speaks to me those words of love. He could no more
grow without me than a vine can grow without its branches.

June 26—Isabel Florence Hapgood, Ecumenist and Journalist

"I stood listening to the melodious intoning of the priest and wondering, for the thousandth time, why Protestants who wish to intone do not take lessons from those incomparable masters in the art, the Russian deacons. That simple music, so perfectly fitted for church use, will bring the most callous into a devotional mood long before the end of the service. [I]t spoils one's taste forever for the elaborate, operatic church music of the West." [10]

"As for what was sown on good soil, this is the one who hears the word and understands it, who indeed bears fruit and yields, in one case a hundredfold, in another sixty, and in another thirty."
Matthew 13:23

Since humans appeared on earth, a force has been at work to create communion. The fruits of human labor are passed on to, developed, and shared with succeeding generations. "It is as if a mysterious bridge is being built throughout the course of time that connects all persons."[11] When Florence Hapgood traveled to Russia to become fluent in the language, she may not have known that she would fall in love with the Russian Orthodox liturgy and make it her life's work to translate it into English. She may not have anticipated that her work would build a bridge of ecumenism during and after the Russian revolution. It is a joy to know that Your word, growing in me, helps You build a bridge between those born before me and those yet to be born, spreading communion, bringing a little closer the time when You are all in all.

---

[10] Isabel Florence Hapgood, *Russian Rambles*, p. 116; *see http://www.gutenberg. org/catalog/world/readfile?fk_files=1511128&pageno=116*[1]
[11] Sofia Cavalletti, *The Religious Potential of the Child 6 to 12 Years Old* (Chicago, Liturgy Training Publications, 2002), p. 35.

June 27

𝕏

"My Father is glorified by this, that you bear much
fruit and be my disciples."
John 15:8

You called Isaiah to be a servant in whom You would be glorified. When Isaiah thought he had labored in vain, You told him that when he was still in his mother's womb You called him by name. Your reminded him, as You reminded Moses, that salvation was not his work but Yours. You promised that he would not fail, and moreover, that his efforts would enable Your salvation to reach the ends of the earth, manifesting in compassionate aid to prisoners, the hungry and thirsty, and all those who suffer. While He was still in Mary's womb, You called Jesus by name to incarnate Your salvation on earth. His Sermon on the Mount echoes Isaiah's prophecies, reassuring Your people that You keep Your promises. "Does a woman forget her baby at the breast, or fail to cherish the son of her womb?" (Is 49:1,15) You called me by name from my mother's womb. How can I glorify You here and now?

June 28

*After Jesus had spoken these words, he went out
with his disciples across the Kidron valley to a place
where there was a garden, which he and
his disciples entered.*
John 18:1

On this night Jesus is the first to enter the garden, the place where human life began and where his human life will end. His entry begins a mysterious process that will transform the garden forever. In this garden, seeds sown in weakness and dishonor will be raised in glory and power to restore once and for all the covenant relationship between You and humanity. Jesus, the new Adam, offers himself to You so that Adam, Eve, and all who have turned away from You, may return. (1 Cor 15:43, 45) His free offering of love is the gate through which all who hear his voice enter the garden to become one flock with one shepherd. (Jn 10:16)

June 29

Now there was a garden in the place where
he was crucified, and in the garden there was a new tomb in
which no one had ever been laid.
John 19:41

"The seed had to die," I told a small circle of three-to six-year-olds as we contemplated John 12:24. Newspaper spread on the floor held the remains of seeds planted four days, one week and two weeks ago. Shoots sprouted from two pots, but the third showed nothing but bare dirt. After carefully dumping out the pots, they eagerly and gently probed the soil. The dead seeds were lost in the presence of burgeoning new life: roots and pale green shoots curled tightly. Someone asked Paul how the dead were raised, with what kind of body. He answered, "What you sow does not come to life unless it dies. So it is with the resurrection of the dead. What is sown is perishable, what is raised is imperishable." (1 Cor 15:42) The imperishable in Jesus was raised and grew into an entirely new kind of life, unimaginably greater, a Vine that encompasses all people of all time and all places. That life is growing in me.

June 30

Jesus said to her, "Woman, why are you weeping?
Whom are you looking for?" Supposing him to
be the gardener, she said to him, "Sir, if you have
carried him away, tell me where you have laid him,
and I will take him away."
John 20:15

*A*s soon as she saw Him, Mary Magdalene knew. In the dim light of dawn her vision was obscured by tears; nevertheless with the eyes of her heart she saw the Gardener. In the garden Eve hid, fearing You; but Mary, mourning the loss of One with whom she loved to walk, went fearlessly in search of You. Were You happy, You who moved heaven and earth to be reunited with Your people? Did Jesus' heart rejoice as He called her by name, "Mary!" and heard her amazed response, "Teacher!"? Like the shepherd who found the sheep, the woman who found her coin, the father who found his son, and Mary, who, on finding the risen Christ, ran to tell the disciples, I long to rejoice with my friends, for my Lord was dead and has come to life; He was lost and is found. (Lk 15:32) Eucharist is the garden in which I meet You and all who are dear to me, a foretaste of the time when my tears will be wiped away, and I will see You face to face.

July:
Learning to Rely on God

July 1

In God alone there is rest for my soul.
Psalm 62:1(a)

Rest for my soul; just thinking about that makes me breathe a sigh of relief. How I long to step off the unrelenting merry-go-round of chores, worries, and obligations, and escape into a rest deeper than a stolen moment in the recliner or the exhausted flop into bed at night. My soul is the most profound, most hidden part of me, and also the most real. While my body changes and will some day drop away, the real me, my soul, will live on, united with You. I don't have to wait to experience that future bliss; I can taste it here and now, whenever I pray the intimate prayer of silent listening, resting quietly in Your love.

July 2

From God comes my safety; with God alone for my rock,
my safety, my fortress, I can never fall.
Psalm 62:1(b)-2

*W*hen I am in trouble and feel like there is no one I can rely on and nothing to hold onto, the idea of holding onto You seems . . . just that, only an idea. But when times are very dark and I realize that the outcome is not something I can control, I know that *all* I can do is pray, and that *all* can seem little indeed. The only one I can rely on, ever, is You. You are the only constant in my world, in which people and things appear and disappear with alarming unpredictability. That *all* that I can do is the only power I have: the power to turn to You, my rock, my safety, and my fortress—the greatest strength I have.

July 3

🙚

Rely on God, people, at all times; unburden
your hearts to God.
Psalm 62:8(b)

*H*ow many times have I felt laden with troubles and wished that I had someone I could tell them to, someone who would listen without judging me and with complete understanding and sympathy? This person would listen patiently, without interrupting, for however long it took me to tell my story. There would be no detail that would not be interesting to my listener; his or her attention would never wander, and interest would never flag. Where, oh where could I find this friend of my heart?

I picture You waiting patiently, watching, not judging me, with complete understanding and sympathy, Your attention never wandering, Your interest never flagging, waiting for however long it takes. . . for me to remember You, the most loving friend of my heart, and tell you my story.

July 4

𝔐

Ordinary people are only a puff of wind,
important ones delusion; put both in the scales and up they go,
lighter than a puff of wind.
Psalm 62:9

Years ago I went to the 35th reunion of my high school. Pulling into the parking lot, I was already comparing: my car to the other cars in the parking lot, my husband to the others in the parking lot. I took a quick, stealthy scan of the women inside and sighed inaudibly with relief as I judged that my figure and clothing fit safely into the middle range. I jealously regarded the women who were slimmer than me and noticed with guilty smugness those who had gained a lot of weight. Petty enough, but I awaited with dread the reintroductions. "What do you do?" The woman whose weight I had smugly compared with mine was vice-president of a management consulting firm. "And what do you do?" "Um . . . I'm an at-home mom." There was no graceful way to bring up the employment I'd left to stay at home, "Well, I used to do something really interesting!" would only make me look, and feel, worse. Help me to remember that my achievements don't win Your love. Help me recall Your words to the prophet, Samuel, "People look at appearances, but God looks at the heart." 1 Sam. 16:7.

July 5

🜨

Though riches may increase, keep
your heart detached.
Psalm 62:10(b)

"*N*o danger there," I think wryly, knowing that any increased riches will go directly to pay our bills. Yet my riches have increased quite a bit since I was a young woman working my way through college. As the riches increased, so did my desire to live in a larger home, own certain things, enjoy better food, and travel to more far-flung places. When I think about not being able to have and do these things, I realize that my heart is far from detached. I am like the praying man in the *New Yorker* cartoon, "God, I do not ask for many things, only that they be of good quality." I have put things into the place in my heart that should be occupied only by You. Things bring pleasure for a little while; then I become bored and want other things. Instead of satisfaction, there is only more wanting. Far from being satisfied, I feel endless longing, even deprivation. I *am* deprived—I'm depriving myself of You. Help me detach myself from wanting things and make room in my heart for the joy of Your love.

July 6

It is for God to be strong, for you,
Lord, to be loving; and you yourself repay us
as our works deserve.
Psalm 62:11(b)-12

When I hear about yet another outrage or injustice, it is hard not to think those people are getting away with it. It's not fair! The cry of my childhood echoes in my head; my neck and shoulders tense, my jaw clenches with frustration. Why doesn't the government do something? Why don't that child's parents do something? Why don't my neighbors do something? I fantasize about taking matters into my own hands. Why, if that happened to me I'd .... Stop. Breathe. Pray. It is for You, not me, to be the strong one, to make decisions grounded in love. It is for You to repay those people, not me. Just...one thing: when you repay me as my works deserve, please do be loving.

July 7

In the way of your decrees lies my joy, a joy
beyond all wealth.
Psalm 119:14

*J*oy is not an emotion I ordinarily associate with obeying Your decrees. Buying things doesn't bring me joy, either. I feel joy when things are going well with the important people in my life, or when I achieve a personal goal that is very important to me. What do Your decrees have to do with either of those? The Bible tells me repeatedly of Your unconditional love for me. When I feel loved, it is easier to love the people in my life, and that brings me joy. The Bible gives me advice about how to treat others, making it easier to know what is the right thing to do. Doing the right thing brings me joy. The Bible helps me know what kind of goals are worth working for, the kind of goals You have in mind for me. Those are the goals that will bring me the most joy.

July 8

✠

God, my heritage, my cup, you, and you only,
hold my lot secure; the measuring line marks out
delightful places for me.
Psalm 16:5-6(a)

Delight: it's a feeling I would like to have more often. The places You mark out for me in life are delightful. I forget sometimes how fortunate I am, how blessed, to be Your daughter. In those delightful places I can drink You in and feel secure. Maybe I should visit You more often! I can do that right where I am when I rest in Your presence and remember Your love for me and all the blessings You have showered upon me. When I look at the beauties of Your creation, both great and small, in their amazing abundance and variety, I am filled with awe, wonder, and gratitude. Why so many different shells? Why are the flowers so beautiful? Why did God bother to create all this? For me.

July 9

Let kindliness and loyalty never leave you:
tie them around your neck, write them on the
tablet of your heart.
Proverbs 3:3

*I*n the bustle of my day I struggle to keep my focus: what is the next thing that has to be done? And the next? And the next? I could get it all done if these people around me would only cooperate. Darn that driver, that lady who has 20 items in the express check-out lane, that child who is arguing with me instead of doing what he knows he is supposed to do! It can feel like an obstacle course. "Let kindliness and loyalty never leave you." The psalmist knows how hard that is and so gives me practical advice. I might really buy a cheap locket and put in it a heart-shaped piece of paper with the words, "kindliness and loyalty." Each morning when I put it on, I will remember.

July 10

Your word is a lamp to my feet, a light on my path.
Psalm 119:105

When I walk in the dark I'm afraid I will stumble and hurt myself. In my house there is an electric light for every room and hallway. Outside, the front and back doors are lit. Our neighborhood is so lit up that the night is never really dark. We do this to feel safe. Inside my mind and heart I can't put an electric light. How can I travel safely on all the paths of life? Your Word is the lamp I've been looking for. It was right here all the time. Reading Your Word helps me move more confidently in its light.

July 11

I thank you, God, with all my heart;
I recite your marvels one by one, I rejoice and exult in you,
I sing praise to your name, Most High.
Psalm 9:1-2

Frequently I am asking You for one favor or another. I'm careful what I ask for. I don't believe I expect too much. Do I? Sometimes I feel that You haven't heard me or have let me down. This psalm makes me think: how often do I thank You? Do I ever take time to remember all the gifts that You have given me, much less tell anyone else about it? Help me take time today to think about all You have done for me. Most of all, never let me forget Your limitless love for me, which is no abstract love, but palpable, concrete, and shown in so many ways. I can find joy in each day if I take time to thank You and exult in Your love.

July 12

*Your love is before my eyes, and I live my
life in loyalty to you.*
Psalm 26:3

*H*ow easy it is in summer to see Your love before my eyes.
Each leaf, each flower, is a miracle of beauty. The flower pours
out its heart in radiance, perhaps never seen in its short life
by anyone but You. Help me to be inspired by the flower's
example and let my inner beauty radiate in response to Your
love. By that effort, I will live my life in loyalty to You.

July 13

Avert my eyes from lingering on inanities,
give me life by your word.
Psalm 119:37

*Y*esterday, the psalm reminded me that Your love is always before my eyes. How much time do I spend each day distracted by inanities, the silly, stupid things constantly calling for my attention on TV or the radio, in magazines at the grocery store, and in gossip? How much time each day do I spend on Your Word? Which focus brings more light and joy? The psalm provides the answer: Your Word gives me life.

July 14

✻

Trust in God and do what is good . . . make
God your only joy.
Psalm 37:3(a),4(a)

𝒯rust in God. It sounds simple, but it's not. Life is hard and complicated and it's not always easy to know what is the good thing to do. I pray, and sometimes things don't turn out the way I want them to. I suffer, or someone I care about suffers; happiness in life is a fleeting thing. What does it mean to trust in You? The Bible tells me that You are faithful; I can rely on You to carry me through good times and bad. I carry out my part in our relationship when I pray and try to do good. The joy comes in the time I spend with You. When joy seems lacking in my life, help me remember to spend more time with You.

July 15

*Be strong, let your heart be bold, all
you who hope in God!*
Psalm 31:24

The psalmist encourages me. When I hope in You, I am able to be strong and let my heart be bold. I do hope in You. But how often do I take encouragement from that hope? So often when I pray, I passively wait for You to make something happen in my life. This line from the psalm is a little startling. Help me remember this day and every day that my hope in You gives me the power, even the duty, to be strong, to act boldly from my heart in all I do.

July 16

⚜

Now guide me with advice.
Psalm 73:24(a)

*W*ouldn't it be great if, at the beginning of every day, I could know Your advice for what to do that day! My worries and confusion would disappear. My confidence would soar. Or maybe not. Here is Your Word on my table . . . and it remains there, usually closed. How eager am I to learn Your advice? When I read Your Word, does my confusion disappear? No. I'm an adult now, with an adult's intelligence and responsibilities. You are relying on me to do my part in bringing Your salvation to the world. The choices of each day may seem small in the big picture, but they are no less important, and rarely easy. Your advice is at my fingertips to guide me in those choices. They light my path, but I must take the steps.

July 17

✠

Thus says God who made you, who formed
you from the womb, who is your help:
Do not be afraid.
Isaiah 44:2

*H*ow many times have You told me do not be afraid? These words appear countless times in the Bible. So why am I so anxious? Why do I worry so much, day after day? My prayers are full of worries, full of requests, and light on praise. In my anxiety for things to turn out the way I want them to I have forgotten You. Or maybe I don't trust You, and think I can do a better job of controlling things. Only You are God, and I... I am Your creation. You love me and help me. When I trust and follow you, I can let go of my fear.

July 18

🎕

Happy the one who cares for the poor and sick;
if disaster strikes God will come to help.
Psalm 41:1

When I think about caring for the poor and sick, "happy" is not the first word that comes to mind; more like "duty," "chore," or "burden." If a family member gets well, then I am happy. But sometimes they don't get well. Add "sad" and "angry" to the list of words. On the other hand, when I help make food for the homeless with our group at church, I always leave feeling better about myself than before.

The Bible doesn't say that disaster won't strike, only that You will help me when it does. When disaster came to me people did help me and I knew that help was from You. I don't think it's a *quid pro quo*—I help others, so You help me—but more of an awakening on my part to how You work your saving help through us, Your people. When I help others, I am more open to receiving help when I need it.

July 19
Feast of St. Macrina the Younger

"The soul should know herself accurately and should behold the Original Beauty reflected in the mirror and in the figure of her own beauty. For truly herein consists the real assimilation to the Divine - making our own life in some degree a copy of the Supreme Being."[1]

—*Macrina the Younger*

So God created humankind in God's image,
in the image of God he created them
male and female he created them.
Genesis 1:27

*H*ow can I know myself accurately? Sometimes I feel confident, loving, and beloved. Sometimes I feel worthless and abandoned. And how can I be sure that I am not deceiving myself? Perhaps I can start by looking in the mirror and reminding myself that You created me in your own image and likeness. I reflect You, the Original Beauty. Help me to remember that truth each day and to care for myself so that Your beauty shines out in me always.

---

[1] *In Her Words*, p. 57.

July 20
Feast of Elizabeth Cady Stanton

*"Whatever the Bible may be made to do in Hebrew or Greek,
in plain English it does not exalt and dignify woman."* [2]
—*Elizabeth Cady Stanton*

*The woman saw that the tree was good to eat . . . and
that it was desirable for the knowledge that it could give.
So she took some of its fruit and ate it. She gave some also to her
husband who was with her, and he ate it.*
Genesis 3:6

Other than Mary, the Mother of God, it's hard to find a
woman that the Bible holds out as a role model for humanity.
There is Sarah, Esther, and Mary Magdalene, the first
disciple (frequently confused with a different woman who
was a prostitute). Jesus had women disciples, and women
were leaders and martyrs in the early church. Maybe it's not
so hard. People blame Eve for the fall of humankind, when
the Bible states plainly that Adam was with her when she
decided to eat the fruit of the knowledge of good and evil.
What a fine example of the "superior sex" Adam is, standing
there without a word to say, silently cooperating in the Fall!
Come to think of it, most of the men in the Bible aren't so
exalted and dignified, either. Jacob cheated his brother out
of his birthright. King David wanted another man's wife,
so arranged to have him killed in battle. Peter denied Jesus
three times. Let's face it: we are all weak, yet You love us
more than we can ever know. Thank You for loving me, just
the way I am.

---

[2] *In Her Words*, p. 319.

July 21

But I, so great is your love, may come to your house.
Psalm 5:7(a)

*I*magine the house of God! If You lived in a real house, what might it look like? In my imagination it is filled with light and love, laughter, music, and beauty, like a wonderful party to which I am longing to be invited. And I am invited! You invite me constantly to live with You there in intimate relationship. You invite me to be at home in Your love, to share in Your joy. It's an invitation I can accept any time I wish, in a place as close as my heart, where You dwell within me. Help me to accept Your invitation today.

July 22
Feast of St. Mary Magdalene

🖾

*Jesus said, "Woman, why are you weeping? Who are you looking
for?" Supposing him to be the gardener, she said,
"Sir, if you have taken him away, tell me where you have put
him, and I will go and remove him." Jesus said, "Mary!"
She knew him then and said to him in Hebrew,
"Rabbuni!" – which means Teacher.
John 20:15-16*

Sometimes I picture myself in the place of Mary Magdalene,
standing distraught at the empty tomb of my beloved
Jesus. Through my tears, I see a man approach, a stranger,
interrupting my private grief. Startled, I can't imagine who he
could be. The gardener, perhaps? His voice is compassionate.
Maybe he knows where the body is? Then I hear him call
me by name with that unmistakable voice of love. Only this
time, it's *my* name. And in that moment, my whole world
changes forever.

Each day, You call me by name with that tender love.
Whatever my mood, let me always answer You with joy, and
remember that You have changed my life forever.

July 23

🦋

Oh, for the wings of a dove to fly away and find rest.
Psalm 55:6

*A*men! Whoever wrote that must have had days like some of mine, days of feeling overwhelmed and not up to the task. Days of feeling like no one understands and no one cares. Days when the best thing I could think of to do was to stay in bed hiding under the covers. I longed to find rest, *real* rest, someplace I couldn't get to on my own, where all my challenges were far behind me. I'd need the wings of a dove to get to that place. Luke's gospel says that Your Spirit has the wings of a dove. If only You could help me escape on those days. But Jesus' life shows that escape isn't Your way. You, who are the Way, show me what to do when life's challenges seem to threaten my very existence: shoulder my burdens and follow You, my Good Shepherd, who leads me through the gloomy valley. With You, I lack nothing.

July 24

🎔

*In love there can be no fear, but fear is driven out by perfect
love: because to fear is to expect punishment,
and anyone who is afraid is still imperfect in love.*
1 John 4:18

So I am still imperfect in love; what else is new? Sometimes
Your Word seems to be coming from another planet. Who
is free of fear? Maybe a saint or two. Isn't there a line in the
Bible somewhere that the beginning of wisdom is fear of You?
What gives? Now that I have gotten that off my chest, what
could these words be saying to me about my relationship with
You? Your love for me is perfect, and therefore You do not
fear me, nor do You fear *for* me. That's a comforting thought.
You don't worry about me the way I worry about the people
I care about, the way I worry about whether You really love
me. You trust me and trust our journey together. You know
we are going to be all right. Knowing that, maybe I could
learn to trust You a little more and let my fear gradually fade.
Maybe I could lose that old "hellfire and damnation" story
and start to trust that Your great love rejoices in my imperfect
efforts to love You.

July 25

※

For I am certain of this: neither death nor life, no angel, no
prince, nothing that exists, nothing still to come,
not any power, or height or depth, nor any created thing,
can ever come between us and the love of God made
visible in Christ Jesus our Lord.
Romans 8:38-39

This is a hard one for me to comprehend. I like to see, hear, and touch the people that I love. I experience Your love through the love of people, right? And things—events, sickness, death, estrangement, etc.—have come between me and some of the people who I have loved. So how is Your love different? Right now, one of the people I love is halfway around the world away from me. Has that distance reduced my love for him? A woman who's love saved my life is dead. After she died, I didn't know whether I could live without her. Slowly, I grasped the fact that through her love of me, she became part of me. She lives within me in some mysterious way. That's what love is like between You and me. I don't so much believe in Your love as experience it. Your love is something that happens to me, whether I notice it or not. Help me to notice.

July 26
Feast of St. Anne, mother of Mary,
the mother of God

As you live, my lord, I am the woman who stood
here beside you, praying to God. This is the child I
prayed for, and God granted me what I asked.
Now I make him over to God for the whole of his life.
1 Samuel 1:26-28

*W*hen I prayed for a child and gave birth I was both overjoyed and overwhelmed. What a tremendous responsibility was on my shoulders; almost too great to comprehend. Each hour of the day my first thought was for *my* baby, who soon grew to become *my* child, who soon grew to become . . . . an adult; still my child and yet, inescapably, not mine anymore. I'd heard the truism that our children don't belong to us, that we have them for a while and then let them go, but the reality of it hit me like a sucker punch. Its a painful truth. Help me find comfort in remembering that, although my child does not belong to me, she does belong to You.

July 27

Raise me up when I am most afraid.
Psalm 56:3(a)

*H*ere is an image that resonates: cowering in fear. When I am most afraid my impulse is to hunker down at home with the doors locked, preferably under the covers in my bed. Unfortunately, these are usually the times I have to face with courage, for example, when someone I love is in danger. I'm long past the age at which I believed hiding under the covers will make the bogey-man go away, yet I'm no less terrified to come out and face him down. There's a good reason for the old saying that there are no atheists in foxholes. Thank You for being there for me when I fearfully whisper, "Help me, God!" Raise me up day by day to trust in you so that the next time fear strikes and threatens to pull me down, I can stand courageously as I call Your name.

July 28

This I know: that God is on my side.
Psalm 56:9(b)

*I*n my head I hear a simple song I learned in my childhood, "Jesus loves me, this I know, for the Bible tells me so." So simple, even simplistic, yet it kindled in me a ray of hope that You were not some terrifying old judge in the sky, watching for me to make one false move so You could strike me dead. The Bible is filled with words that tell of Your love for me. Yet that is only part of the story. I know You are on my side because I experienced the truth of Your Word in my life in the midst of trials so difficult I didn't know how I could survive them. Relying on Your Word, I prayed to You, then put my head down and walked, turning neither to the left nor the right, but straight ahead through those terrible storms in blind reliance on Your protection. How about those other people, the ones who were making life so hard for me? You are on their side, too, but that's another prayer.

July 29
Feast of Mary and Martha,
sisters of Lazarus

🎴

*If you had been here, my brother would not
have died.*
John 11:21,32

*H*ow often I have thought this! Where were You when the one died who I loved so dearly? Its interesting that neither Martha nor Mary ask the "why" question, the question with no answer. Their question is less an accusation than a statement of faith: You have the power to bring new life to the dying; even to the dead. Martha follows up with an even more powerful statement: "Yes, Lord, I believe that you are the Christ, the Son of God, the one who was to come into this world." What her words must have meant to You, knowing, as You did, the agony that lay ahead! May I follow Martha's and Mary's example and trust that my loved ones have not died, but live in You.

July 30

*I call on God the Most High, on God who has
done everything for me.*
Psalm 57:2

*W*hen I think about it in a certain way, I've got a lot of guts
calling on You. Reading the Book of Job or Christ's Passion,
I see that I'm not dealing with some kind of pastel fairy
godmother who will make my every wish come true. Yet . . .
when I think of all You have done for me I am overwhelmed
with humility and gratitude. Who am I that You should
create all this for me? So much beauty! So many gifts, most
often taken for granted. How often do my prayers imply: so
what have You done for me lately? Yet You never stop giving,
and You never stop inviting me into intimate relationship
with You.

July 31

✤

My heart is ready, God, my heart is ready.
Psalm 57:7(a)

When did I know my heart was ready to accept Your invitation into intimate relationship with You? It's not something I knew with my head. No one could have told me. There was a feeling of quiet joy and anticipation, a gradual realization that there was nothing else more interesting to me than You. I began making time for You each day. I heard Your name in a crowded room. I read Your Word as if it were a love letter written especially for me. You called and called and called and I finally heard, answered You, and fell in love. You'd think that would be it, happy ever after, but I'm ashamed to admit that I have gone for days—weeks—immersed in my own worries and forgetting to take time alone with You. Help me heed Your call of love, and make time each day to enjoy our love together.

August:
Dwelling in the Kingdom of God

August 1

What is the kingdom of God like? And to what
should I compare it?
Luke 13:18

*I*magine Jesus' dilemma: sent by You to invite us to a place
indescribable, yet as familiar as as our beating hearts. I picture
Jesus saying to You: "So . . . what do I tell them?" and Your
answer, "Oh, I don't know . . . you'll think of something." Jesus
looks around and sees: a mustard seed, the size of a piece of
dust, that grows into the largest shrub, becoming shelter for
every kind of bird; a woman mixing tiny grains of yeast into
flour to create dough that rises, as if by magic, to become food
for many. He sees seed decaying on parched, bare ground,
and later, a waving cornfield; here: death, there: through Your
creative power, life. Out of the most insignificant beginnings
You create your mighty kingdom. Open my eyes and heart;
help me discover Your kingdom in which I dwell.

---

[1] Jeremias, J., *The Parables of Jesus*, Prentice Hall, 1972, pp. 148-9.

August 2

✷

The kingdom of God is not coming with
things that can be observed; nor will they say, 'Look here it is!' or
'There it is.' For, in fact, the
kingdom of God is within you.
Luke 17:20-21

The kingdom of God is within me?! What a puzzling and exciting announcement. Wow! How could I have missed it? Maybe I've been searching in the wrong places, like when I look everywhere for glasses that are on my nose. I pray for this thing or that, looking blindly for something that seems out of reach. "If only God would just give me what I ask for everything would be okay" Please help me remember to stop . . . breathe . . . and tune in to Your kingdom, right where I am.

August 3

🦢

*The disciples asked, "Who is the greatest in the
kingdom of heaven?" He called a child to him and set
the child in the midst of them. Then he said, "Truly I tell you,
unless you change and become like children you will never
enter the kingdom of heaven. Whoever becomes humble
like this child is the greatest in the kingdom of heaven."
Matthew 18:1–4*

What a surprise this must have been to the disciples! What
a bewildering paradox to be presented with not an adult, but
a child. What is it about a child that makes her my model?
A child is vulnerable, a quality that scares me. A child is
open and receptive. She observes the world without preconceptions and with wonder and awe. She has an innate
dignity. She loves with her whole being and is capable of a
profound response to Your love. So what are You asking me
to do? To reclaim the me who is vulnerable, who is open
and receptive to Your love. To dismantle my accumulated
preconceptions and allow myself to experience wonder and
awe in Your kingdom. To be humble: to risk losing face by
embracing my innate dignity as Your child. To accept Your
love and respond with my whole being. Give me the courage
to become like a child.

August 4

🜨

The kingdom of God is as a man might throw seed on the soil.
Night and day, while he sleeps, when he is awake, the seed is
sprouting and growing; how, he does not know. On its own, the
soil bears fruit: first the shoot, then the ear,
then the full grain in the ear.
Mark 4:26-28

*I*t's true: I prepare the ground, I plant the seeds and water them, but I cannot make the seeds grow. Some seeds don't grow, but the ones that do . . . . they always amaze me. I'm like a child again, eyes wide, mouth open. Wow! How does that happen? There are other kinds of seeds that I plant: work, children, and other relationships. They don't all grow either, but the ones that do - do they amaze me? Or am I too busy evaluating them to enjoy the wonder of their miraculous growth? Am I too worried about whether they are growing the way I want them to, and how they reflect on me? Help me remember that I can plant and tend the seeds in my life, but only You can make them grow. Help me rediscover my childhood awe and wonder at the miracle of growth in Your kingdom.

August 5

*The kingdom of heaven is like a mustard seed which a
man took and sowed in his field. It is the smallest of all the seeds,
but when it grows it is the biggest shrub of all and
becomes a tree so that the birds of the air come and
shelter in its branches.*
Matthew 13:31-32

The biggest shrub of all? That image doesn't exactly conjure
up a picture of triumph. Why not the biggest tree of all?
Maybe size isn't the point. Maybe triumph isn't the point,
either. What is the payoff here? Shelter for all the birds
of the air. That word shelter is often used in the psalms to
describe You. "You who live in the shelter of the Most High,
who abide in the shadow of the Almighty, will say to the
Lord, 'My refuge and my fortress; my God, in whom I trust.'"
(Ps 91:1-2). Hmmm. But Jesus says that Your kingdom is
like, not the fully grown shrub, but the tiny seed; in Israel,
mustard seeds are as tiny as a speck of dust! How could Your
kingdom be like that seed?

August 6

※

*The kingdom of heaven is like the yeast a woman took
and hid in three measures of flour till it was
leavened all through.*
Matthew 13:33

*I*n yesterday's reading, Jesus compared Your kingdom to a seed as tiny as a speck of dust. Today, he says Your kingdom is like yeast, also very tiny in its separate grains, and hidden when it is mixed in with flour. There's a pattern here. What happens when yeast is mixed with flour into a dough? The yeast disappears, and the dough rises through some mysterious force. Jesus says that Your kingdom is like that yeast. Could Your kingdom really be that tiny? What is that yeast that Jesus is talking about? And what happens when that force is mixed into something, like my life?

August 7

*The kingdom of heaven is like treasure hidden in a field
which a man found and hid; then in his joy he goes and
sells all that he has and buys that field.*
Matthew 13:44

There's that quality of hiddenness again, although a treasure is not tiny like the seed and the yeast. I feel like I'm on some kind of treasure hunt, tracking down the clues to discover what is this kingdom of Yours. Here, Jesus compares Your kingdom to a hidden treasure, buried in a field not owned by the searcher. I can imagine the man's overwhelming joy, a joy so intense that selling his other possessions is a mere task to be performed in order to possess the source of that joy. Jesus seems to say that this joy is available for me, as well. But how can I find it? I need more clues.

August 8

*Again, the kingdom of heaven is like a
merchant in search of fine pearls; on finding one pearl of great
value, he went and sold all that he
had and bought it.*
Matthew 13:45–46

*R*ight after the parable about the hidden treasure, Jesus tells this parable about the merchant in search of fine pearls. There is some connection between them. Pearls, like treasure, are worth a lot. In Jesus' time, before pearls could be cultured, they were fabulously expensive, almost beyond imagining. This merchant found a pearl that was worth so much he sold everything he had to buy it. Jesus seems to compare the man who found the treasure with the merchant who found the pearl, implying that, on discovering the one pearl, the merchant felt the same overwhelming joy as the man who discovered the treasure. Pearls are also very beautiful. Beauty brings me joy. Overwhelming beauty, such as I've found sometimes in nature, has brought me overwhelming joy, and awe and wonder. Could that beauty be within me?

August 9

Your kingdom come, your will be done,
on earth as in heaven.
Matthew 6:10

*I*s this a prayer or an announcement? Jesus is teaching us how to pray, yet, coming from him, this sentence reads like a statement: Your kingdom is come and Your will is done on earth as it is in heaven. When I pray this line from the *Our Father*, I understand it as my plea: let Your kingdom come and Your will be done on earth. Something else that I'm curious about: is Jesus saying that whenever Your will is done, that means Your kingdom is come—or vise versa? Either way, this is exciting news: Your kingdom is here as it is in heaven! Amen.

August 10

Repent, for the kingdom of heaven
is close at hand.
Matthew 4:17

When I was a child, I saw a television show during which, every 15 minutes or so, an old man with an absurdly long beard and wearing a robe and sandals would walk through the scene calling out, "Repent! Repent!" holding a sign with the same message. The audience laughed. I thought it was a ridiculous notion that the world would end any time soon. I have since learned that there are many ways in which a person's world can end: the end of a relationship, loss of a job, illness, and death are a few situations that might cause a person to feel or express sincere regret or remorse. Why would the nearness of Your kingdom be a reason to repent? I've learned that paying attention to the wrong things keeps me from seeing Your kingdom. It makes sense that doing the wrong things takes me away from life in Your kingdom, to a world of my own where I forget about You. That really would be the end of the world! I repent of all the distractions in my life. Help me stay focused on Your kingdom.

August 11
Feast of St. Clare of Assisi

From The Rule of St. Clare: *"The sisters are to keep silence . . . . . However, they may briefly and quietly communicate what is really necessary always and everywhere."* [2]

When words are many, transgression is not lacking, but the prudent are restrained in speech.
Proverbs 10:19

*W*ords can hurt or heal. Silence can hurt or heal. How to know when to speak and when to keep silent? One might think St. Clare's sisters had it easy because they had her Rule, but there is her ending instruction to speak "what is really necessary always and everywhere." They still had to judge for themselves what You would have them do in any given moment of the day or night. How to know what is prudent, what will show care and thought for the future? Your Word holds clues: avoid many words; aim for restraint in speech. St. Clare's Rule helps me understand that word "restraint": silence is the default setting; and I need to notice what is going on around me. Necessary, in Your kingdom, means the loving action, the action that serves Your purposes, in as few words, and as quietly as possible. St. Clare's Rule seems like a good guide for my life.

---

[2] *In Her Words*, pp. 132-33.

August 12
Feast of Florence Nightingale

"I never see a soap bubble when I am washing my hands without thinking how good God was when He invented water and made us invent soap. He thought of us all and thought how He could make the process of cleansing beautiful, delightful to our eyes, so that every bubble should show us the most beautiful colours in the world. It is an emblem of His spirit, when we put our own into it and handle them too roughly; immediately they break, disperse and disappear. So I try to put as little of my own as possible into things." [3]

— Florence Nightingale

God, what variety you have created, arranging everything so wisely! Earth is completely full of the things you have made.
Psalm 104:24

Now here is a woman who lived in Your kingdom! Florence Nightingale heeded Your call to heal others and made it possible for countless others to do the same. But the thing I love about her is that she saw You in every soap bubble. She knew where to look for the kingdom of God! She paid attention to the right things. If I could do that, I would see You day and night; I would never lose sight of You. If You are in every soap bubble, I can barely imagine all the places You can be seen. Grant that today I will see You everywhere I look.

---

[3] Letter/draft/copy to Sir Harry Verney 12 May 1890, Add Mss 45791 ff211-13. http://www.uoguelph.ca/~cwfn/spirituality/franciscan.html

August 13

The mysteries of the kingdom of heaven
are revealed to you.
Matthew 13:11

Something that has been revealed to me should no longer be a mystery; nevertheless, here I am, almost two weeks into August, and I still don't know what Your kingdom is. What have I learned so far? Jesus says that the kingdom is hidden; it is within me; it is like a seed that grows on its own, without help from me; it can be entered only by those who become like children; it is like the tiniest of seeds that grows to become a large shrub, a shelter for all; it is like tiny grains of yeast that invisibly cause dough to rise; it is like a hidden treasure or one precious pearl that cause overwhelming joy; it is on earth as it is in heaven; it is available to those who repent of actions not in accord with Your will. In all of his teachings, Jesus didn't try to define Your kingdom; he described a force beyond our knowing. Maybe knowing isn't important to You; maybe the important thing is living.

August 14

*I am telling you not to worry about your life
and what you are to eat, nor about your body and how you
are to clothe it. . . . Set your hearts on God's kingdom,
and these other things will be given you as well.*
Luke 12:22, 31

This is one of those sayings of Jesus that seem so unrealistic that it could apply only to saints. How am I supposed to get food and clothing for myself? I can't think of anyone who would give it to me, day in and day out. What do You expect me to do? Give up everything and hope for the best? What?! Oh . . . you're not telling me not to think about those things, only not to worry? What about obsessing; is obsessing okay? No? I didn't think so. If I spent half the time thinking about Your kingdom that I do about food and clothing, I probably would be a saint. But I see you don't want me to think about Your kingdom, You want nothing less than my heart. Ah. When was the last time someone asked me for my heart? So, this is love? Yes.

August 15
Feast of the Assumption of Mary

*I shall immortalize your name, nations will
sing your praises for ever and ever.*
Psalm 45:17

$\mathcal{B}$lessed Mother, I celebrate and praise you for your faith and heroism. You overcame your doubts about the impossibility of the angel's announcement and accepted the risks so that humanity could be saved. When you said "yes" to God you became co-creator and allowed God to become a child within you. You have been called the model disciple. No one can repeat your act of perfect selfless devotion, but, inspired by your example, I can echo your answer to the angel Gabriel and say to God, "I am Your servant; let what You have said be done within me."

August 16

Ask, and it will be given you; seek, and you
will find; knock, and it will be opened to you. For everyone who
asks receives, and everyone who seeks finds, and for everyone
who knocks, it will be opened.
Luke 11:9-10

Jesus seems to be saying that Your kingdom is a place that must be sought to be found;   a place enclosed where one must knock to enter. I picture You waiting behind that door, with bated breath, holding Your pearl, Your treasure: Your kingdom, like a diamond engagement ring in your trembling hands, hoping against hope that I will accept your invitation, seek You out, knock, and ask for that gift. I do.

August 17

*Let the little children come to me and do not stop them;
for it is to such as these that the kingdom of heaven belongs.*
Matthew 19:14

My children's well-being is my constant concern. Don't I make sure they are in the best schools possible? Don't I check their homework and drive them to endless activities? Don't I wonder whether they will have any social skills, since they seem to relate best to their electronic devices? Don't I insist that they go to church with me? Um... well children *are* a nuisance in church, moving around and making noise when they're not supposed to, disturbing and embarrassing me when all I want is one place where I don't have to deal with them, so I can concentrate on my prayers. Is that too much to ask?

August 18

It is easier for a camel to pass through the eye of a
needle than for a rich person to enter the kingdom of God."
When the disciples heard this they were astonished. "Who can be
saved, then?" they said. Jesus gazed at them. "With men," he
told them, "this is impossible; with God everything is possible.
Matthew 19:24-26

*W*hen I hear that last sentence read in church, I always add bitterly to myself, "That's not true." Blasphemous? Well, how else to account for some of the horrific things that have happened to the people I love even while I was praying to You? If everything is possible for You, why did you allow us to suffer so much? Why didn't you save us? When you didn't answer my prayers I thought You didn't love me. Now I believe You love me but I still hold a grudge against You. I have doubts. I'm still angry at You; yes, after all this time, and after all my efforts to understand and to heal. All Your efforts to show me You love me haven't taken away the pain. Do I want the pain to go away? Would I have to let go of my grudge, my last defense against You? What if I let myself love You completely? What will happen then?

August 19

Many who are first will be last, and the last first.
Mark 10:31

Good! I can think of some people I'd like to see brought low. There are also ones I'd like to see raised up: the handicapped, the abused, the poor; so many people who never had a chance. Where do I fit on the scale? What a person is in the eyes of the world doesn't necessarily count in Your kingdom. I don't know if You even have first and last people. There's Mary, and the disciples and saints, but somehow I don't think Your love can be measured on a scale of one to ten. Anyway, what does it matter to me whether I am first or last, as long as You and I are together?

August 20

❧

*Blessed are the poor, for yours is the
kingdom of God.*
Luke 6:20

*F*or most of my life, I assumed that the poor would enjoy
this blessing only in the heaven of my childhood, somewhere
"up there." I couldn't imagine that the poor could enjoy Your
kingdom on earth. Most of my experience with the poor
is with my brother who is mentally handicapped and the
people he lives with. They possess nothing. They suffer to
an extent I can only guess at. How is Your kingdom within
them? (As I write, I realize they and them mean not like me.
How is your kingdom within my brother? By turns, he might
be listless and withdrawn, or restless. Sometimes when I sit
with him holding his hand, I feel how contented we are
together. Sometimes, when he first sees me, his eyes blaze
with joy and love so intense that it amazes and unsettles me.
I force myself to meet his gaze and try, weakly, nervously, to
return the almost superhuman love that pours out of him, for
a few moments, like a fire hose. Is that it? Could it be that he
knows Your love that powerfully?

August 21

Jesus said, "The blind see again, the lame walk, lepers are cleansed, and the deaf hear, the dead are raised to life, the Good News is proclaimed to the poor and blessed is the one who does not lose faith in me."
Luke 7:22-23

This is heaven, not those silly pictures of humans with wings and halos walking on the clouds, but real people, sick and handicapped, are healed, even the dead brought back to life! You gave no vague promises of a better life hereafter to people suffering here and now; Your love for us is such that You came among us on earth, healing and announcing Your good news to the people who needed it the most. Still not satisfied, You allowed Jesus to endure death and then raised Him so that His risen life could be spread among all people of all times and all places; even me. I feel blessed to hear the good news that You bring healing and new life to people on earth as it is in heaven.

August 22

Jesus sent them out to proclaim the kingdom
of God and to heal the sick.
Luke 9:2

*A*m I, too, sent to proclaim Your kingdom and to heal? I've learned that in Your kingdom, how I live is more important than what I say. Your kingdom is within me, but does my life proclaim Your kingdom to those around me? I'm not a doctor or a nurse, so how can I heal? There are wounds that aren't in the body, but in the mind or heart. Sometimes I get so angry at a person, I wish that something bad would happen to them. One time, a crowd brought to Jesus a woman caught in adultery. Under the law, she could be stoned to death. Trying to trick him, people in the crowd asked Jesus what he thought they should do to her. He said that the one among them who was without sin should throw the first stone. One by one they all went away until Jesus and the woman were alone. He asked the woman, "Has no one condemned you?" "No one, sir," she replied. "Neither do I condemn you." Jesus said, "Go and sin no more." Please heal my wounds. Let my life proclaim Your compassionate love.

August 23
Feast of St. Rosa de Lima

✠

"And I saw [Jesus] face to face a very long while . . . face to face, all entire, from feet to head. And from His face and body, there came to my spirit and my body rays and tongues of glory so that I thought myself ended with this world and in glory itself." [4]
- Rosa de Lima

For now we see in a mirror, dimly, but then we will see face to face. Now I know only in part; then I will know fully, even as I have been fully known.
1 Corinthians 13:12

*S*t. Paul articulates two of my deepest longings: to see You face to face, and to know You fully, even as I have been fully known. Those last words jump out at me. I long to be fully known by those I love. At least, I think I do. Maybe its just as well that the only one who knows me fully is You. On the other hand, I'm probably the only one fooled by my "I'm okay" act. Psalm 139 says "you examine me and know me" - and You still love me! I do long to see Your face, Jesus, even though the thought is a little frightening. St. Rosa was so in love with You that she could face You joyfully and fearlessly. Banish fear from my heart; let me rest assured that I am fully known, and loved, by You.

---

[4] De Sola Chervin, Ronda, *Prayers of the Women Mystics,* Servant Publications, Ann Arbor, MI, 1992, p.134.

August 24

There will be more rejoicing in heaven over
one repentant sinner than over ninety-nine virtuous
people who have no need of repentance.
Luke 15:7

Okay — as long as that one repentant sinner is me. I can tell Jesus is talking about Your kingdom because in real life we don't treat repentant sinners very well. Ex-convicts are pretty much marked for life; many of them can't get any but the most menial work, if that. Many become homeless. Just the word "ex-con" says it all for most of us. How about "homeless person"? I'm okay with making meals for them or helping run the shelter, but I don't want to sit next to one on the bus. If I heard that my new neighbor was formerly homeless would I welcome her with open arms? I know You would want me to. I pray for the grace to welcome and rejoice over each person in Your kingdom as You have welcomed and rejoiced over me.

August 25

*Not all those who say to me, 'Lord, Lord,' will enter the
kingdom of heaven, but the person who does the
will of my Father in heaven.*
Matthew 7:21

This reminds me of when my children were little. "Mommy!
Mommy!" they would cry. I heard it so often. I could usually
tell by the sound of their voices when they really needed me,
and when they were nagging me for something they wanted
me to do for them or buy for them. When that happened I
would turn one deaf ear until they became distracted or got
tired of nagging. When they did what they were supposed
to do, like their homework or their chores, I tried to let them
know that I appreciated everything they did in school and to
make our family life better. I tried to give them what they
needed. Your Word tells me everything I need to know to
live in Your kingdom. Today, instead of asking you to give me
what I want, I will reflect on Your word and try to do Your
will, trusting that You will give me what I need.

August 26

Once the hand is laid on the plow, no one who
looks back is fit for the kingdom of God.
Luke 9:62

*J*esus said this to someone who wanted to follow Jesus but first say good-bye to his people at home. Jesus seems hard here, not the welcoming Good Shepherd who searches tirelessly for the lost sheep. There's an urgency to His message: there is no time to lose. When I think of the coming of Your kingdom in its fullness, the time when You will be all in all, it seems very distant; certainly not in my lifetime. Jesus contradicts this, telling me that not even a day can be wasted. I wonder whether the work I do helps bring Your kingdom. Today, give me the courage to take a good, hard look at what I do every day. Help me to do the work You would have me do to help Your kingdom come on earth—soon.

August 27

No one can see the kingdom of God without
being born anew.
John 3:3

A teacher in my Catholic high school invited me and a group of classmates to a Pentecostal prayer meeting. There, people would lay their hands on me, say some words in a language I couldn't understand, and - presto! - I'd be born again, healed, and made happy from then on, sort of like Sleeping Beauty after the prince's kiss. I saw other girls go through it and emerge, smiling, with what I privately called their glassy-eyed stare. Traditional Catholicism didn't include this ritual, but my family was going through a terrible time and, depressed and frightened, I thought, why not? Afterwards, I waited for the miraculous transformation but felt nothing. In the school chapel I knelt, trying to figure out why the prayer ritual didn't work on me. "God must not love me," I thought, bleakly. I thought I would have to live without You, and so went on with life, thinking, like a toddler with her hands over her eyes, that if I couldn't see You, You couldn't see me. The day I realized that I was mistaken, that You were with me all along, the day I realized that I never stopped living in Your kingdom, is the day I was born anew.

August 28

People will come from east and west, from
north and south, and will eat in the kingdom of God.
Luke 13:29

*I*n the parable of the Good Shepherd, Jesus, who was a Jew preaching to Jews, said there were also "other sheep not of this fold" that he had to bring, that they would become one flock with one shepherd. (John 10:16) Sometimes I hear about a religious figure pronouncing judgment on one person or a whole group of people. Recently, a group was convinced that the end of the world was coming on a certain day, and that anyone who did not profess that group's particular brand of Christianity would be "left behind." I don't concern myself with the question of who will be saved and who will not. All who have gathered at the eucharistic feast eat it in Your kingdom.

August 29

*The kingdom of heaven can be compared to
ten bridesmaids who, having taken their lamps, went
out to meet the bridegroom. Five of them
were foolish and five were wise.
Matthew 25:1-2*

*J*ust when I think I've got this kingdom thing figured out,
Jesus throws me a curveball. At the end of the parable of the
Ten Bridesmaids, the foolish ones, who neglected to bring
oil for their lamps, say, "Lord, lord, open the door for us."
and the bridegroom answers, "Truly, I do not know you."
This reminds me of the earlier reading in which Jesus talks
about people who say, "Lord, lord . . ." but have not done
Your will. Could the oil represent the actions I do in accord
with Your will? In doing Your will, could I fulfill that duty
for someone else? When I worry about someone not doing
Your will, maybe I am not trusting that You invite them just
as You invite me into intimate relationship with You. Maybe
I think I'm one of the wise ones and they aren't. Help me
trust you to take care of others and focus on filling my own
lamp so it can burn bright.

August 30

For not in speech is the kingdom of God but in power.
1 Corinthians 4:20

𝒫aul spent his life preaching and writing the good news, yet he admonishes me not to be swayed by all who call themselves preachers of Your gospel. He says I am not to look for Your kingdom in words, but in power. In what can I see Your power? There is the mysterious power of the seed that grows into a large shrub. Who could make that seed grow? There is the power of the yeast to make a heap of flour and water triple in size and become food for many. Who could make that yeast grow and raise the dough? Who could make a pearl so beautiful and valuable that it changes a person's life? Who could create the human being, a microscopic speck that grows into a person capable of relationship with You? Humans are the instruments of healing, but who is the source of all healing power? Paul reminds me not to be distracted by humans who say they know all about You, but to keep my focus on You, the source, the power that creates Your kingdom.

August 31

If, because of food, your brother or sister is grieved,
you are no longer walking in love... For the kingdom of
God is not food and drink but righteousness and peace
and joy in the Holy Spirit.
Romans 14:15, 17

*F*inally, words that describe life in Your kingdom in a tangible way: above all, I need to walk in love. Love includes righteousness and peace and joy. Haven't I always longed for this life? Haven't You engraved it on my heart? Is this what it means to have Your kingdom within me? Just before the Israelites entered the promised land, You told them, "For this Law that I enjoin on you today is not beyond your strength or beyond your reach. It is not in heaven, so that you need to wonder, 'Who will go up to heaven for us and bring it down to us, so that we may hear it and keep it?'... No, the Word is very near to you, it is in your mouth and in your heart for your observance." (Deut 30:11-12, 14) Let me always live so.

September:
Changing Seasons

September 1

There is a season for everything, a time for
every occupation under heaven:
Ecclesiastes 3:1

On its face this sounds optimistic, like a public relations slogan. "Everything" is a good thing when we're talking about "everything on sale," but the writer of Ecclesiastes is not an optimist. In my life every type of experience will have its time: good, bad and indifferent, and I won't have much choice about that. Are things bad now? Don't worry, they'll eventually get better. Are things good now? Don't become complacent; bad times will come. It's a truth that I'd better learn to live with, and even see as a blessing. Give me the courage to live in Your truth, whatever the season.

September 2

※

A time for giving birth, and a time for dying;
Ecclesiastes 3:2

Yesterday a friend died: a mother, good-humored, smart and vivacious. We used to be catechists to the children in our church. For Jesus' parable about the grain of wheat (Jn 12:24) we planted seeds and let them grow. Two weeks later, we read the parable and . . . then let the children dig up the seeds. They had disappeared, but under the soil we saw what had been hidden from view: a new plant being born. We said, "The seed had to die. If it wasn't in the earth, all this growth would not have taken place." That force within the seed is in my friend. What new life, hidden from view, are You bringing to birth in her?

September 3
Prudence Crandall

*"I have had in the Providence of God to pass through many
trying seasons but place them all together they are of small
moment compared with the present scene of adversity — yet in
the midst of this affliction I am as happy as at any
moment of my life . . . ." [1]*
– Prudence Crandall

*Happy are you when people abuse you and persecute
you and speak all kinds of calumny against you on my account.
Matthew 5:11*

*A*voiding adversity seems sensible. I spent years holed up
alone in my apartment after work, day after day. I can't say I
was happy, but I succeeded in not being hurt. One day, an old
friend walked into our office to apply for a job. She invited
me to share an apartment with her and another friend. Soon
I took other risks: going back to school, dating, getting
married, having a baby: each one brought some adversity, yet
I felt happier than at any moment of my life thus far. Thank
You for giving me the courage to discover the mysterious and
intense happiness that arises only in the face of adversity.

---

[1]Prudence Crandall, "Letter to Simeon Jocelyn (April 17, 1833)," published in
"Abolition Letters Collected by Captain Arthur B. Spingarn," *Journal of Negro
History,* vol. XVIII, 1933, p. 82-84.

September 4

*a time for planting and a time for uprooting what
has been planted.*
Ecclesiastes 3:2

*W*hen I raise tomatoes from seed I plant many seeds in order to get enough plants. What tremendous joy I feel when the seeds sprout and grow! But the seedlings will not grow into tomato plants unless they are thinned out. How hard it is to uproot my precious seedlings. In my life, I sometimes plant more seeds than I can handle. When I have too many commitments none of them can grow well and, worst of all, they crowd out my time with You. Today, give me the courage to begin uprooting some of the commitments in my life so that the important ones can grow and thrive.

September 5

A time for killing and a time for healing;
Ecclesiastes 3:3

Before his death, Jesus tells the disciples that he must be killed and then raised on the third day. Peter reacts, "This must not be!" but, far from being touched by Peter's concern, Jesus tells him, "Get behind me, Satan! You are a stumbling block to me; for you are setting your mind not on the things of God but on the things of men." (Mt 16:23) On the other hand, Jesus healed people and even raised them from the dead. How to reconcile this apparent paradox? Jesus says I need to set my mind on Your "things." What things? "Seek first the kingdom of God and God's righteousness, and all these things will be added unto you." (Mt 6:33) Let that be my prayer as I make difficult choices.

September 6

a time for knocking down and a time for building.
Ecclesiastes 3:3

*W*hen His disciples showed Jesus the temple, which they believed housed Your very presence, He said, "Truly I say to you, there will not be one stone upon another here which will not be demolished." (Mt 24:2) They wondered how You could be present among Your people without the temple. John explains that when Jesus spoke about the destruction and raising up again of the temple, He was speaking of the temple of His body. (Jn 2:21) Jesus' prediction came true: the temple was demolished, but not until after Jesus was "knocked down" so that a new understanding of Your presence could be built. Today, let my life reflect the truth of what the nuns used to say: my body is a temple of Your Spirit.

September 7

A time for tears and a time for laughter;
Ecclesiastes 3:4

Right before His passion, Jesus tells His disciples that there will be a time for tears and a time for, if not laughter, joy. "You will be weeping and wailing ... but I shall see you again, and your hearts will be full of joy, a joy that no one will take from you." (Jn 16:20-22) He speaks of a woman giving birth who grieves because "her hour has come," but when she gives birth to the child she forgets her affliction "because a man is born into the world." When I gave birth, I wasn't grieved so much as terrified, as well as joyful. What can birth teach me about my life with You? When Christ rose, a new kind of man was born into the world along with a new kind of joy. In the midst of my times for tears, let me not forget the joy that is mine forever.

September 8

a time for mourning and a time for dancing.
Ecclesiastes 3:4

Jesus' parable of the forgiving father, Luke 15, tells of the son who takes his inheritance while his father is still alive, and squanders it until he is destitute and starving. He returns, confessing, "Father, I have sinned against heaven and before you." The father orders a feast to celebrate. The party is in full swing when the elder, loyal son returns home, and he angrily refuses to join the celebration. He might be wondering, "Does my father love my brother more than me? Why have I bothered to obey and please him all these years?" When a situation seems unfair I feel angry and hurt, and it's hard to see the joy in life. When I wonder whether I am loved, help me remember that Your answer is always "Yes."

September 9 - Constance,
Superior of the Sisters of St. Mary, and her companions

🕮

When an epidemic of yellow fever struck Memphis in 1878, Sr. Constance and three other Episcopal nuns stayed in the city to tend to the sick and dying, despite the high risk of contracting the disease, which often resulted in a painful death. Known as the Martyrs of Memphis, Constance and her companions are memorialized in the Episcopal Calendar of Saints.[2]

"Anyone who wants to save his life will lose it; but anyone who loses his life for my sake, and for the sake of the gospel will save it."
Mark 8:35

*M*artyrdom: it's a word I associate with grisly tales of saints being thrown to the lions or burned alive in the bad old days before Christianity became accepted, normalized, and safely boring. The story of Sr. Constance and her companions, who stayed in Memphis, Tennessee, to care for people dying of malaria, reminds me that martyrdom did not end with the Roman empire, and Christianity is not safe, not if I take it to heart like Constance did. And if I don't take it to heart, am I living my faith or just using it as a security blanket? If I lose the safe life I pretend to have, will I like the life I save: the real life I have with You?

---

[2] http://en.wikipedia.org/wiki/St._Mary%27s_Episcopal_Cathedral_in_Memphis#Constance_and_her_companions

September 10

A time for throwing stones away and a time for
gathering them up;
Ecclesiastes 3:5

*F*oreshadowing His own resurrection, Jesus said at Lazarus' tomb, "Take the stone away." . . . and the dead man came out. (Jn 11:39, 44) He also said, "The stone that the builders rejected has become the cornerstone." (Mt 21:42) The stone thought to establish forever the finality of death is revealed as the keystone of the kingdom of God, bringing life without end to all creation. What does such a grand concept have to do with You and me? What apparent barrier in my life is a stepping-stone to deeper relationship with You?

September 11

a time for embracing and a time to refrain from embracing.
Ecclesiastes 3:5

*W*here in the New Testament is the time for embracing? Jesus' instruction to the disciples to "love one another as I have loved you," (Jn 15:12) seems to ask only a brotherly care of each other. While it's liberating to know that I don't have to get married, I don't see any affirmation for married love, only implications that marriage is for sissies. Let them try it! In the Old Testament there is time for embracing: Adam has Eve, Abraham has Sarah, Isaac has Rebekah, etc. Paul says only that it is better to marry than to be aflame with passion. (1 Cor 7:9) But who created this heart aflame and these arms that crave embrace? How else would I have any idea how much You love me?

September 12

A time for searching and a time for losing;
Ecclesiastes 3:6

*J*esus tells about the lost coin, the lost sheep and the prodigal son who was lost to his family. How could losing, or being lost, be a good thing? The woman and shepherd did not give up searching, the father did not give up watching and waiting, until the coin, sheep, or son was found. At the end of each search, there was a party to celebrate their reunion. I can identify with the lost sheep and the prodigal son, but what about the ones who lose? Did the woman need to lose the coin? Did the shepherd need to lose the sheep? Did the father need to lose his son? Is there something or someone that I need to lose in order to be reunited even more joyously than before?

September 13

🜚

a time for keeping and a time for throwing away.
Ecclesiastes 3:6

*J*esus said to keep Your commandments and to throw away
anything that prevents that - even an eye or a hand! When
someone asked Him what is the greatest commandment, He
said, "You shall love God with all your heart, all your soul and
all your understanding." (Mt 22:37) How can I give You all
my heart, soul and understanding when I have so many other
commitments? I can't just throw them away. When Jesus'
disciples left their families to follow Him, who do You think
took care of all those people? May I not give you a heart that
loves, a soul that lives, and understanding that struggles right
where I am?

September 14

a time for tearing and a time for sewing;
Ecclesiastes 3:7

There is an ancient gesture of tearing of one's clothes in grief. When Jesus gave up His spirit on the cross the curtain of the temple was torn "from above to below in two," (Mt 27:50-51) as if You tore Your robe in grief. The prophet Hosea foresaw such a moment of tearing, and also the moment of sewing, or binding, beyond it:

> Come, let us return to the Lord;
> for it is he who has torn, and he will heal us;
> he has struck down, and he will bind us up.
> After two days he will revive us;
> on the third day he will raise us up,
> that we may live before him. (Hos 6:1-3)

What in my life needs to be torn, then healed and bound up again, so that I may live before You?

September 15

a time for keeping silent and a time for speaking.
Ecclesiastes 3:7

*I*n the gospels, when someone discovers who Jesus is, He orders them to keep silent. After His resurrection, when the time for speaking has come, Jesus instructs the disciples, not to say who He is, but to "proclaim the Good News to all creation." (Mk 16:15) Jesus seems to say, "It's not about me." What is He getting at? "For this I was born, and for this I came into the world, that I might testify to the truth." (Jn 18:37) The truth is, without You, I can't speak the truth. Today, help me know when to speak and when to keep silent so that my life can proclaim Your good news.

September 16

A time for loving and a time for hating;
Ecclesiastes 3:8

"*H*ate evil and love good." (Am 5:15) It sounds like the moral thing to do, but Jesus says, "You have heard it said, 'You shall love your neighbor and hate your enemy.' But I say to you, love your enemies and pray for those who persecute you, so that you may become children of your Father in heaven, for he makes the sun rise on the evil and the good." (Mt 5:43-45) Maybe the time for hating is over. Easier said than done, yet I know that hatred has never done me any good. Help me to let go of hatred today and live in Your time, the time for loving.

September 17 - Hildegard of Bingen

*"I sensed in myself wonderfully the power and mystery of secret
and admirable visions from my childhood - that is,
from the age of five - up to [the age of 42], as I do now."* [3]
- Hildegard of Bingen

*"I thank you, Father, Lord of heaven and earth, because you
have hidden these things from the wise and the intelligent and
have revealed them to children."*
Matthew 11:25-26

*I*t seems strange that wise and intelligent people could fail
to know what a child knows. Countless theologians and
religious people over thousands of years have spent their lives
studying You. Endless words have been written and spoken
about Your Word. Yet a child's comment can reveal You to
me so profoundly that I am amazed and wonder, where did
that come from? Next time I hear words of wisdom from a
child, help me to stop and listen carefully, remembering that
You speak directly to her heart.

---

[3] *Mystics of the Christian Tradition*, p. 83.

September 18

a time for war and a time for peace.
Ecclesiastes 3:8

*I*n the gospels, the word "war" never comes out of Jesus' mouth. The word "peace" appears in his speech approximately 22 times. He was a disappointment in the role of Messiah because he was not the warrior king that people were hoping for. There is so much talk of war; even events that are not wars are framed in those terms: the war on poverty, the war on drugs, the war on obesity, etc. What if we declared peace on our challenges instead of declaring war, not the peace of collusion, but the peace that allows us to stop fighting and cooperate? Today, when I am tempted to declare war on someone, help me to declare peace.

September 19

*God did not leave you without evidence of himself in the good
things he does for you: giving you rains from heaven and
fruitful seasons, and filling you with food
and your hearts with joy.*
Acts 14:17

Shortly before His death, Jesus gives final instructions
to the disciples. Couched within advice and warnings He
says, "I have said these things to you so that my joy may be
in you and your joy may be made full." (Jn 15:11) Amid a
bewildering, even terrifying, series of announcements, Jesus
says that the point of it all is joy. What might He have felt,
knowing the horror to come, and also knowing that at the
end of it joy would be established forever through His risen
life? Help me face my trials, remembering all the good You
do for me, with trust that the fruit they bear will be joy.

September 20

🙐

*God said, "Let there by lights in the vault of heaven to divide
day from night, and let them indicate
festivals, days and years."*
Genesis 1:14

One of the things I love about You is that You understand
the need for parties. During the first three days of creation,
You created the environment and the food; on the fourth, You
created the decorations: the moon and stars. Your purpose for
the sun, moon and stars was nothing so prosaic as survival;
no, they were to show us when to have parties. When I get
too bogged down in the daily grind, help me remember what
Your priorities are.

September 21

*Has the sight of the sun in its glory, or the glow of the moon as
it walked the sky, stolen my heart, so that
my hand blew them a secret kiss?*
Job 31:26-27

When was the last time I was enchanted by the sight of
the sun or moon? Has my heart become so hardened? Am
I so jaded by the endless parade of human-made wonders
that Your miraculous creation has ceased to move me? True,
where I live, surrounded by buildings, it is hard to see the
moon for more than a couple of hours at night, and the stars
are all but invisible. The sun in summer can be obscured by
a toxic haze. I tend to rush from destination to destination
in my climate-controlled car. Today, and tonight, help me
remember to stop, look, and let my heart be stolen by Your
glorious creation.

September 22

❧

At his will the south wind blows, or the storm from the
north and the whirlwind.
Ecclesiasticus 43:16-17

"*A*nd suddenly from heaven came a sound like the rush of
a violent wind . . . and all were filled with the Holy Spirit."
(Acts 2:2, 4) In Hebrew, the word for wind also means spirit.
Whenever the wind blows, Your Spirit is blowing over the
earth, through the trees outside my window, brushing my
cheek and messing up my hair. Today, remind me to take a
moment to feel Your Spirit filling me with grace and courage:
as available, and as necessary, as the air I breathe.

September 23

In the same way, his treasuries open and the clouds
fly out like birds.
Ecclesiasticus 43:14

*I*n poetry and song, clouds are often portrayed as a bad omen or a metaphor for sad times. The writer of Ecclesiasticus has another way of looking at clouds: they are Your gifts. Without clouds there would be no rain; without rain there would be no crops; the earth would become a dust bowl, uninhabitable. Maybe the events that seem like clouds in my life are really gifts, escaping like birds from Your treasuries, so that something new may grow in me.

September 24

*The cold wind blows from the north, and ice forms
on the water, settling on every watery expanse,
and water puts it on like a breastplate.*
Ecclesiasticus 43:20

*W*hat would my life be like without winter? Sitting on my screened porch in August I anticipated the end of summer with dread. Fall is beautiful, if a tad melancholy, but winter! I shiver just thinking about it. Is Your Spirit in the cold wind? What are You bringing me, besides ice and snow? Along with more time spent indoors, there is more time for reading and reflecting on Your Word. Along with increased darkness, there is more time for candles and tea. While the garden outside sleeps, my inner garden is alive; You wait there for me.

September 25

*He sprinkles snow like birds alighting, it comes down
like locusts settling. The eye marvels at the beauty of its
whiteness, and the mind is amazed at its falling.*
Ecclesiasticus 43:17–18

How poetically the writer expresses the experience of
watching snow fall! I, too, am amazed and delighted at the
first snowfall, before resigning myself, martyr-like, to the
drudgery of winter. This fall let me not dread the coming
of winter. Instead, when the snow covers the ground like a
flock of white doves may I see, not a burden, but Your Spirit
renewing the face of the earth.

September 26

"He scorches the desert, like a fire he consumes the vegetation.
But the mist heals everything in good time,
after the heat falls the reviving dew.
Ecclesiasticus 43:21-22

John the Baptist foretold that Jesus would baptize with the Holy Spirit and with fire. Jesus warned that those who do not remain in him are like withered branches, cut off and burned in fire. On the day of Pentecost, tongues of fire appeared above the heads of the disciples. Your fire consumes and purifies, while the waters of baptism heal and revive us. When I feel burned by betrayal, or consumed with anger or grief, help me be open to receive the reviving dew of Your healing, and so grow stronger in Your love.

September 27

The sand of the sea and the raindrops, and the
days of eternity, who can assess them?
Ecclesiasticus 1:2

*D*ays of eternity. For a few moments, let me try to imagine the unimaginable. Along with the sand and the raindrops, I am an exceedingly tiny part of Your vast creation. The idea is humbling and somehow comforting; that I am part, however small, of a very big picture gives me a share in its grandeur. I genuflect to You in recognition that You are great and I am small. Yet You know the number of hairs on my head. Today, I am grateful for the days of eternity. As one season follows another, You and I have plenty of time to get to know each other.

September 28 - Margery Kempe

"Then for joy that she had and the sweetness that she felt in the dalliance [conversation] of our Lord, she was in point to 'a fallen off her ass' [donkey], for she might not bear the sweetness and grace that God wrought in her soul." [4]
- from The Book of Margery Kempe

Pleasant words are like a honeycomb, sweetness to the soul and health to the body.
Proverbs 16:24

$\mathcal{M}$argery Kempe's reaction to You reminds me of another holy woman who fell off her mount. Rebekah traveled a long distance to meet Isaac, her betrothed, for the first time. When she saw him walking through the fields toward her, she fell off her camel, then hid her face behind a veil. (Gen 24:64-65) Theirs was the rare biblical marriage of true love. Margery swooned, not at the sight of You, but at the sweetness of Your words. "Amazing grace, how sweet the sound, that saved a wretch like me . . . ." That song will run through my head today.

---

[4] *The Norton Anthology of English Literature,* 6th Ed. Vol. 1., New York: W. W. Norton & Company, 1993, quoted in Luminarium: Anthology of English Literature, http://www.luminarium.org/medlit/kempe4.htm.

September 29

May the name of God be blessed for ever and ever,
since wisdom and power are his alone. His, to control the
procession of times and seasons.
Daniel 2:20-21

Summer is over; Fall is here. I can't help but wonder, is there just an endless cycle of seasons, or are we moving towards some goal? Paul says that from the beginning You had a hidden plan "to act upon when the times had run their course to the end" to bring everything in heaven and on earth together under Christ. (Eph 1:10). On that day I'll be reunited with loved ones who have gone back to You, and with those who have not yet been born; all of us together, with You. That's a plan I can live with, beginning now.

September 30

🜨

Thanks to him all ends well, and all things hold together by means of his word.
Ecclesiasticus 43:26, 28

*A*ll's well that ends well. Seasons come and go, but not indefinitely. In the words of Julian of Norwich, "All shall be well, and all shall be well, and all manner of thing shall be well." [5] Your Word holds all things together - how? In his letter to the Colossians, Paul says of Jesus, "in him all things hold together. He is the head of the body . . . For in him all the fullness of God was pleased to dwell." (Col 1:17-19) I give thanks that, through Jesus, You are pleased to dwell in me so that all shall be well, no matter the season.

---

[5] *http://en.wikipedia.org/wiki/Julian_of_norwich*

October:
Harvesting

October 1

An angel came out of the sanctuary and shouted aloud,
"Reap: harvest time has come and the harvest
of the earth is ripe."
Revelation 14:15

You would think I could notice when a field, genuine or metaphoric, is before me, ripe and ready for harvest, yet an angel is shouting at me, "Reap!" Am I asleep? What could this unseen harvest be that is staring me in the face? Why does the angel need to startle me? What are You waking me up to?

October 2

"The kingdom of God is as if someone would scatter seed on the ground, and the seed would sprout and grow, he does not know how. When the crop is ready, he loses no time: he starts to reap because the harvest has come."
Mark 4:26-29

*Y*esterday, I wondered what the harvest is and why You are sending an angel to shout at me. Now I see that it has something to do with Your kingdom, and it is important to pay attention. If I had been alert, like the man in this parable, I would be ready and would not need an angel to startle me. Something that, like seed, has been scattered and has grown mysteriously must be reaped without delay. Help me to see what has grown in my life and is ready for harvest.

October 3

🕎

The Lord said to Moses, "I am going to rain bread from
heaven for you, and each day the people shall go out
and gather enough for that day."
Exodus 16:4

*A*h! That seed that was scattered on the ground, could it be
bread from heaven? After the Exodus, the Hebrew people
wandered in the desert with You as their guide and protector.
They asked for food, so You rained bread from heaven which
they gathered each day in order to continue their journey.
What is the bread you send me each day so that I may
continue my journey with You?

October 4

If you obey the commandments, loving the Lord your
God and serving Him with all your heart and soul,
you shall gather in your new grain and wine and oil,
and you shall eat your fill.
Deuteronomy 11:13–15

*J*esus said that the greatest commandment is to love You with all my heart, soul and strength, and to love my neighbor as I love myself. When I think of serving You with ALL my heart and soul, I feel small and selfish, unable to accomplish so great a goal. Without Your loving me first, I could never do it. But You do love me, so I will try, believing that in the attempt I will reap the harvest and eat my fill.

October 5

*Now when you harvest the harvest of your land, you are
not to finish-off the edge of your field. The full-gleaning of
your harvest you are not to glean; for the afflicted and
for the sojourner you are to leave them; I am the Lord your God.*
Leviticus 23:22

I'm so busy thinking about MY land, MY crops, MY food
for MY journey with You, I forget that it all comes from You.
It's not my harvest. It's not even my journey alone. I'm one
of the many sheep of Your flock; together, we are fed by You.
When I am harvesting Your field, I will not take everything
for myself. I will save some for the afflicted and the sojourner.
Help me remember that abundance comes from You. Help
me take the focus off of ME and MINE and focus on US
and OURS.

October 6

When you enter the land and you reap its harvest, you shall
bring the first sheaf of your harvest to the priest.
He is to present it to God with the gesture of offering
so that you may be acceptable.
Leviticus 23:10-11

*A*t mass, the priest elevates the bread to You using the gesture of offering, and asks that the offering will make us acceptable to You. You asked the Hebrews to bring the first sheaf of their wheat harvest to the priest. When I offer the first fruits of my effort to you, I remember that all of it, including myself, comes from You. I offer myself back to You along with Jesus, the first fruits of Your harvest. I am Yours and You are mine and all is Thine. Amen.

October 7

*You shall observe the Feast of the Harvest, of the first
fruits of your work, of what you sow in the field; and the
Feast of Ingathering, when you gather in the
results of your work from the field.*
Exodus 23:14, 16

I wonder if the original pilgrims, Puritans who knew their
Bible, had this commandment in mind when they ate that first
meal of celebration with the Native Americans who taught
them how to plant and harvest this land. You command
us not only to offer You our first fruits, but to celebrate the
fact that we can offer them to You. In celebration, bare duty
becomes a loving exchange: a gift of love offered, accepted,
enjoyed, and returned back to the Giver. As I gather in the
results of my work, may I always remember and celebrate
You, who first gave to me.

October 8

✤

*The land shall observe a sabbath of the Lord. You shall
not sow your field or prune your vineyard. It shall be a
year of complete rest for the land. The sabbath of the
land will itself feed you.*
Leviticus 25:2, 5-6

*R*est: I understand the concept, but can always think of
something else I should do. I feel more virtuous if I am
constantly busy, never mind that I'm exhausted. Maybe that's
why you had to command the Hebrews to rest: one day a
week for the people, one year out of seven for the land. How
are we going to eat, they might have wondered. Land that is
not exhausted continues to produce in amounts that can be
stored for the sabbath year. People who are not exhausted
can continue to work and not fall ill. Prudently managed,
their resources allow them to take a break or a vacation. Next
time I think that the world won't turn without me, help me
remember Your commandment to rest.

October 9

🙢

*Those who plow iniquity and sow the seeds of grief reap a
harvest of the same kind.*
Job 4:8

You reap what you sow. This truism seems almost a law of
physics, yet, like a child hiding in plain sight, sometimes I
think You won't see. If I don't report this income, no one
will find out. I'm not speaking to him; if he doesn't know
what he did wrong, that's his problem. I won't tell the buyer
that I got water in the basement last year; I need the money.
When I am tempted to behavior that will hurt someone else
because I think I can get away with it, give me the strength
to do the right thing, whether or not anyone—besides You
—will see.

October 10
Vida Dutton Scudder

✿

*"If prayer is the deep secret creative force that Jesus tells us
it is, we should be very busy with it. There is one sure
way of directly helping on the Kingdom of God. That way is
prayer. Social intercession may be the mightiest
force in the world."* [1]
- Vida Dutton Scudder

*Jesus told them about their need to pray always and
not to lose heart. "Will not God grant justice to his
chosen ones who cry to him day and night?
I tell you, he will quickly grant justice to them."*
Luke 18:1, 7-8

On a wall in our church school a piece of paper said, "The
Lord will be with you ...shortly." "Too true," I thought. We
pray at church every Sunday for those in need; I pray daily,
yet the news sounds relentlessly dire. Sometimes I wonder
whether my prayer is helping anybody. Scudder reminds me
that I am praying for the coming of Your kingdom. Like
a seed, its beginnings are small and hidden, but it carries
tremendous force: the force of life, of love —of You. Today
and every day, help me to pray for the coming of Your
kingdom, and to never lose heart.

---

[1] *Holy Women, Holy Men*, p.632.

October 11

*One who sows injustice reaps disaster, and the rod of
her anger falls on herself.*
Proverbs 22:8

*J*esus showed righteous anger when He drove out those
who were selling and buying in the temple. When I'm
angry, I always feel righteous. I never think that I am sowing
injustice, only that I'm reacting to an injustice done to me or
someone I care about. Don't I have a right to be angry at that
jerk who cut me off on the highway? How does my anger
hurt me? Jesus answers, "Be compassionate as your Father
is compassionate. Do not judge, and you will not be judged
yourselves; do not condemn, and you will not be condemned
yourselves; grant pardon and you will be pardoned." (Lk6:36-37)
Next time my anger flares, help me to stop, breathe, and
remember.

October 12

Sow integrity for yourselves, reap a harvest of kindness.
Hosea 10:12

"If you work honestly, considering the good of others as well as yourself, your efforts will be rewarded with kindness," says the good angel who sits on my right shoulder. The red devil sitting on my left shoulder says, "Kindness is nice but it doesn't pay the bills. Will your friends be kind to you when you're a failure? Take care of yourself first and let others take care of themselves." The Bible's advice sounds good, but does it work in the real world? Jesus said, "My kingdom is not of this world." (Jn 18:36) The Bible does not promise material success if I am honest; it says only that I will reap kindness if I live in integrity. I must choose which world comes first in my life.

October 13

✿

The harvest is past, the summer is ended, and we are not
saved. Is there not balm in Gilead any more?
Jeremiah 8:20, 22

Sometimes the summer ends and there is no harvest. The time when I hoped I would reap the fruits of my efforts comes . . . and goes. My ship does not come in. There is no balm, no comfort to be had; only lonely want. Others seem to have succeeded where I've failed. You seem very, very far away, like a tiny planet winking in the cold night sky, impossibly distant. Where is my harvest? Why haven't You rescued me? "My God, My God, why have you deserted me?" said Jesus on the cross. (Mk 15:34). Resurrection came for Jesus, and it has come for me. Help me remember that no matter how comfortless I feel, no matter how far away You seem, resurrection, like spring, always comes.

October 14

The people who walked in darkness have seen a great light.
You have made their joy increase; they rejoice in your
presence as men rejoice at harvest time.
Isaiah 9:1-2

When a word is repeated in scripture, its meaning is intensified. Here, within one sentence, the word "joy" or "rejoice" is repeated three times. To explain how much joy was felt by the people who walked in darkness, Isaiah compares it to the joy people feel at harvest time. To one with a refrigerator and restaurants down the street, harvest does not seem like such a big deal, but to Isaiah's people, harvest meant that they would live for another year. Living in darkness is like living in a tomb. When that person sees a great light, she is filled with intense joy because she knows she will be able to live more fully in that light. Is that the joy Jesus felt when he was resurrected? Is that the joy that You want to share with me?

October 15 - Saint Teresa of Avila

"Sisters, we realize that the soul of the just person is nothing else but a paradise where the Lord says He finds His delight. So then, what do you think that abode will be like where a King so powerful, so wise, so pure, so full of all good things, takes His delight? I don't find anything comparable to the magnificent beauty of a soul and its marvelous capacity." [2]

- Saint Teresa of Avila

"My soul magnifies the Lord, and my spirit rejoices in God my Savior."

Luke 1:47

I imagine the soul of Mary, the abode of the infant Jesus, as such a place: a paradise of magnificent beauty in which the King prepared to be born into the world. Could my soul be anything like Mary's? Teresa says that my soul is a paradise where You dwell, waiting for me. Help me learn to be still and discover my beautiful soul. I long to cling to You and "sing for joy in the shadow of your wings." (Ps 63:7-8)

[2] *In Her Words,* p.224.

October 16

Those who sow in tears shall reap with songs of joy.
Psalm 126:5

There are tears and tears. There are the tears I shed because something happened that was accidental or unavoidable. Then there are tears I shed because of something I chose to do, knowing it would cause sadness, because it seemed I must do it in order to avoid a worse harm. Sometimes there are no good choices; one way or the other, I will cry. I pray to You, then do what I have to do, sowing in tears, hoping I'm right. Have I taken up my cross to follow You? Only You can say. I walk on in prayer, trusting that You will guide me rightly, hoping that the time of my singing is not too far ahead. (Song 2:12)

October 17

*"Look around you, look at the fields; already they are ready
for harvest! Already the reaper is bringing in the
grain for eternal life, and thus sower and
reaper rejoice together."*
John 4:35-36

*L*ate in April, after months of fixing my eyes firmly downward
in order to avoid slipping on ice, I need to remind myself that
it is safe to look up again. I feel as if I've been living in a cave
for the past three months. In winter I go into survival mode:
shoulders hunched, eyes down, one foot in front of the other,
with the world-view of Eeyore the donkey. Lent, which we
celebrate in late winter, suits this mood perfectly but Easter
startles, almost offends me. You mean, all the time I was so
downcast, this new life was preparing to appear and now I
have to celebrate it? Any time of year, when the harvest is
ready, open my eyes and my heart to see it and join in the
rejoicing.

October 18

"The harvest is great but the laborers are few, so ask the
Lord of the harvest to send laborers to his harvest."
Matthew 9:37-38

*W*hy would Jesus ask me to ask You to send laborers to do Your work? Can't You send all You want without my asking? In the parable of the wedding feast, the king calls those who were invited but they will not come. (Matt. 22:3) You invite, You call, but You don't force anyone to follow you. Today I accept Your invitation, follow Jesus to the harvest fields, and pray that others may follow as well.

October 19

❦

*"I sent you to reap a harvest you had not worked for.
Others worked for it; and you have come into the
rewards of their trouble."*
John 4:38

The Bible transports me 2,000 years ago or more to those ancient people who struggled to be faithful to You. I don't often think about the people who struggled to be faithful to You during the intervening 2,000 years. When I do, my 20/20 hindsight makes it easy to evaluate them and judge whether they were successful or not; as successful as, say, me. Jesus reminds me that, were it not for those countless faithful ones, I would not be privileged to have my work set out before me like waves of golden wheat, waiting to be reaped. Today, I give thanks to You for the generations of faithful ones who have done Your work.

October 20

In doing good, let us not lose heart, for we will reap at
harvest time if we do not give up.
Galatians 6:9

*I*t is easy to feel overwhelmed by the problems in my world;
much more so in The World. At times I'm tempted to
conclude with Ecclesiastes that "all is vanity and a chasing
after the wind." (Eccl 1:14) Just as I have reaped the benefits
of others' work, those who come after me will reap a harvest
from seeds I sow. Though I will not receive the benefits of all
the good I do, Paul tells me that a harvest will be mine. Give
me the heart to continue working for Your kingdom.

October 21

A harvest of righteousness is sown in peace by
those who make peace.
James 3:18

Making peace doesn't seem like a good way to gain righteousness. The winning of righteousness requires power and domination, while making peace connotes passivity and capitulation. Many seem to think that fighting is the only means to righteousness. Jesus makes peace by peacefully and fearlessly submitting to authority while asserting Your greater power. When I try to harvest righteousness, give me the courage to seek it by making peace.

October 22

�֍

One who supplies seed to the sower and bread for food will
supply and multiply your seed for sowing and increase the
harvest of your righteousness.
2 Corinthians 9:10

Of course, You are that One who supplies the seeds of righteousness. What are these seeds? Jesus said that the seed is Your Word. (Lk 8:11) In the parable of the sower, some seed fell on rock and withered; some fell among thorns and choked; some fell into rich soil and produced its crop a hundredfold. The sower did his part by sowing; he couldn't make the seeds produce. You also give me bread. Jesus said, "I am the bread of life."(Jn 6:35) When I wonder whether my efforts will bear fruit, help me remember that You have given me both Your Word and Jesus, the bread who sustains me. If I do my part, You will bring the harvest.

October 23

The one sowing sparingly will reap sparingly; the one
sowing for a blessing will reap a blessing.
2 Corinthians 9:6

$\mathcal{P}$aul asks the Corinthians to give money they have promised before he visits them, "as a voluntary gift and not as an extortion." Each fall my church asks me to pledge a fixed amount of money for its support. This is sometimes called "giving back." In true capitalist fashion, I'm tempted to pledge an amount that seems to reflect what I've received from the church in the past year. Paul reminds me that in Your kingdom the laws of giving and receiving are reversed. Instead of deciding how much to give based on what I've received, I will receive an amount that reflects what I've given. Give me the courage this year to sow a blessing.

October 24

𝕏

*The people were reaping the wheat harvest in the plain
when, raising their eyes, they saw the ark and
went joyfully to meet it.*
1 Samuel 6:13

The ark of God, which represented Your presence among the Israelites, had been captured by the Philistines. When the ark was returned, there was great rejoicing. To paraphrase Isaiah 9:2, they rejoiced in your presence as they rejoiced at harvest time. The Israelites knew that each harvest was a gift from You: the miracle of the grain of wheat a million times over. Yet the great joy they felt at harvest was only a foretaste of their overwhelming joy upon the return of Your presence among them. When You seem to have gone away, help me remember that, like the harvest, the time of joy in Your loving presence will come again.

October 25

*"The bread of God is that which comes down from heaven
and gives life to the world. I am the living bread
which has come down from heaven."
John 6:33, 51*

The first bread that came down from You was manna that gave life to the Hebrews after You freed them from the bondage of slavery, and after their miraculous crossing of the Red Sea. Jesus is the bread that came from You to give me life; I who have been freed from the bonds of sin and death through Baptism. Each time I receive You in the bread at Eucharist, You give me life for the week to come. You remind me that I cannot be enslaved by anyone or any thing, because You freed me to live life to the full, here and now. May I always accept the harvest that is mine for the taking, the bread of life that awaits me in Eucharist.

October 26

"I am the vine, you are the branches. Whoever remains
in me, with me in him, bears fruit in plenty."
John 15:5

When I remain in You, and You in me, I am the harvest.
Since I am a branch on the vine that is Jesus, I am already
in You. I don't need to do anything but stay. You are in me
because You created me, because I am baptized, because I
receive You in Eucharist. All those ways, You are in me. The
prayers that I say, the people who I love, the work that I do:
all is harvest for You. I thank you for this reality, and pray
that the harvest of my life brings You much joy.

October 27

*But now Christ has been raised from the dead, the first
fruits of those who have died.*
1 Corinthians 15:20

*A*t the Feast of the Harvest ancient Israelites offered the
first fruits of their harvest to You, an annual ritual to make
them acceptable to You. Jesus is the first fruits of another
harvest. Like the grain of wheat, He was apparently dead—
but wait, look again—He is alive and more fruitful, bearing
a new kind of life. Through Him, we are that field of wheat,
once scattered and dead, now alive: golden fields of waving
stalks, miracle upon miracle, as far as the eye can see. You
are the sower and Jesus, the first fruits, is the One through
whom we are harvested to live forever with You. There are
no words adequate to thank You. May my life be a hymn of
praise.

October 28

As long as earth lasts, sowing and reaping, cold and
heat, summer and winter, day and night shall cease no more.
Genesis 8:22

Sowing and reaping, cold and heat, summer and winter, day
and night. "Night and Day," Cole Porter's song, captures the
rhythm of life. Sung on one repeated note, the words of its
introduction mimic the relentlessness of daily life: the tick
of a clock, the drip of rain drops, the beat of a drum. It has
the sound of destiny: "a voice within me keeps repeating you,
you, you." It could be obsession—or it could be You, You,
You, giving me second, third, or one hundredth chances. Day
after day, with relentless fidelity, You invite me into intimate
relationship with You. Help me to hear and answer Your
siren call.

October 29

When the plants came up and bore grain, the weeds appeared as well. The slaves said, "Do you want us to go and gather them?" But he replied, "No, for in gathering the weeds you would uproot the wheat along with them."
Matthew 13:26, 28-29

*H*ow often have I abandoned a project because some part of it was not working the way I planned, or a person involved was not doing what I wanted? How much time have I wasted doing nothing rather than work that was not up to my expectations? Voltaire said that the best is the enemy of the good. He also said that every person is guilty of the good she did not do. Give me a discerning heart to know the good and the patience to see it through, weeds and all.

October 30

He has made known to us his plan for the fullness of time, to gather up all things in Christ, things in heaven and things on earth.
Ephesians 1:9-10

Slowly, over generations, You have prepared for the day when I read these words of hope. Using the ordinary miracles of creation: light, rain, earth, seasons and seeds, You prepare me for Your harvest. I see you reach toward me, stretching out your finger as You stretch it toward Adam on the Sistine Chapel ceiling. We reach for each other, straining towards the inevitable moment, already but not yet. Christ bridges the gap; He is the ladder of Jacob's dream. Help me cling to Him and so be gathered to You forever.

October 31

*On this mountain, the Lord God of Hosts will prepare
for all peoples a banquet of rich food, a banquet of fine wines,
of food rich and juicy, of fine strained wines.*
Isaiah 25:6

This is how I picture heaven: everyone sitting around a table gorgeously decorated, lit by celestial light, eating the best food and drinking the finest wine, with You, the bridegroom who has arrived at last. So much light! So much joy! Eucharist gives us a taste of the banquet to come, when our longing will cease, our hunger and thirst will be satiated and we see You face to face. For what reason is the harvest if not a feast? When I sit down to eat today, may I remember that You are always there with me, inviting me to taste the heavenly banquet there and then.

November :
Giving Thanks

November 1— All Saints Day

They walked in the heart of the flames, praising God
and blessing the Lord.
Daniel 3:24

*I*sn't this what saints do? Martyr or not, they walk into the fire of faith, joyfully giving their lives to You, and praising You for the chance to do so. What kind of person chooses that life? All those saints seem a little crazy, not able to live a normal life. Or maybe I'm the crazy one, missing out on joys beyond my imagining. Maybe the choice not to be a saint is, like the choice not to be an artist, a failure of imagination, or courage, or lack of faith. Let my weaknesses not limit my love for You.

November 2— All Souls Day

*All the people shouted aloud the praises of the Lord, since the
foundations of the Temple had now been laid. Many who were
then old and had seen with their own eyes the earlier Temple
wept aloud, but many others raised their voices in shouts of joy.
And nobody could distinguish the shouts of joy from the
sound of the people's weeping.*
Ezra 3:11-13

The memory of a loved one who has died can conjure up
feelings like these. There is joy that this person existed, no
matter how briefly, and was known and loved, no matter how
incompletely. In direct proportion to that joy is the grief that
the person exists no more. Weeping can express profound
joy, joy that comes from the deepest well of emotion that,
when tapped, often brings up the tears that are also stored
there. When I pray for the souls I am missing today, I will
not be able to distinguish my grief from my joy.

November 3

Miriam, the prophetess, took up a timbrel, and all the women followed her with timbrels, dancing. And Miriam led them in the refrain: "Sing of the Lord: he has covered himself in glory, horse and rider he has thrown into the sea."
Exodus 15:20-21

$\mathcal{M}$aybe I'm not, like the Hebrew people, being pursued by Pharoah, wanting to kill or capture me, but there are people who would like to capture and use me for their own purposes, material or psychological. I'm thankful to You for delivering me from slavery to people who do not have my best interests at heart, and from purposes that are not Yours. I don't have to wait until Sunday to sing a song of thanks to You.

November 4

Hannah prayed and said, "My heart exults in the Lord; my strength is exalted in my God. My mouth derides my enemies because I rejoice in your power of saving."
1 Samuel 2:1

*N*ot all enemies are external. I can be my own worst enemy, unconsciously sending myself messages that undermine my conscious efforts. "You can't do that! You aren't talented enough/smart enough/capable enough/lovable enough. It's too much trouble. You aren't worth it." These messages weaken me. The messages You send strengthen me: "I have loved you with an everlasting love." (Jer 31:3) "As the Father has loved me, so I have loved you; abide in my love." (Jn 15:9) I rejoice in Your power to save me from my inner, as well as my outer, enemies.

November 5

O give thanks to the Lord, for he is good; for his
steadfast love endures forever.
1 Chronicles 16:34

This prayer is repeated many times in the Old Testament. I thought that was curious until I recalled that, back when You met Abraham, the gods were not good; they were capricious and had to be appeased. When he met You, Abraham may have felt that he was the first human on earth to meet a good god. What might life have been like without knowing You, and that You are good? I don't need to use my imagination; I well remember what life was like before I knew You love me. Thank You for being good, for being steadfast, and for loving me.

November 6

*Who am I, Lord God, and what is my House, that you have
led me as far as this?*
1 Chronicles 17:16

*W*hen I need a lesson in gratitude, especially when things
don't seem to be going well, I need only remember what life
was like before I fell in love with You: in a word, bleak. You
have done so much more than cheer me up. Accepting Your
invitation to intimate relationship has brought new meaning
and purpose to my life. You have helped me to sort out what
is worth doing from what is not worth doing, and given me
the courage to discard the latter so that I can do the former
wholeheartedly. When I look back today, my heart is full.
With wonder and awe I echo King David's prayer.

November 7

I thank you, Lord, with all my heart; I recite your
marvels one by one.
Psalm 9:1

*H*ow often do I even think of Your marvels, much less recite them? Henri Nouwen[1] has written about gratitude as a spiritual discipline that requires daily effort. Today I will begin a list of Your marvels and keep it on my computer desktop, adding to it from time to time, at least until Thanksgiving. On Thanksgiving Day I will read the list out loud, if only to myself, and then I will thank You with all my heart.

---

[1]http://acerminaro.blogspot.com/2006/01/quotes-from-henri-jm-nouwen.html

November 8

✾

You prepare a table before me under the eyes of my enemies; you anoint my head with oil, my cup brims over.
Psalm 23:5

Priests, prophets, and kings are anointed with oil. At my baptism, like priests, prophets, and kings, I was anointed to show that I am holy, set apart for a special purpose (the Hebrew meaning of holy) in Your kingdom. Week after week, You prepare the banquet of eucharist for me. I may have enemies, or be obscure or even a failure in the eyes of the world; this one, all-important thing will always be right. My cup of joy overflows.

November 9

*Why so downcast, my soul, why do you sigh within me? Put
your hope in God; I shall praise him yet,
my savior, my God.*
Psalm 43:5

Sometimes, the best I can do is to have faith that one day,
I will feel thankful. It is at those times that I wonder if You
are as all-powerful as I was taught to believe. It seems the
psalmist is familiar with this feeling; there are a number of
psalms in which the writer acknowledges Your power and
Your steadfast love, and asks, "so why don't You save me?"
The psalmist understands that hope is the beginning of
better times. Refusal to hope closes the door. Expressing my
hope in You opens the door for You to help me. No matter
how sad I feel, let me never close the door on You.

November 10

Blessed be God, who neither ignored my prayer nor
deprived me of his love.
Psalm 66:20

*W*hen that long-prayed-for event happens, I know You heard my prayer and answered me. "God is good!" I proclaim. When the long-prayed-for event does not happen, well, let's just say I have my doubts. Here, the psalmist all but admits wondering whether You would ignore prayer and deprive a person of Your love. In the church of my childhood, a person with such doubts would be considered an unbeliever. Now that I know You better, I believe You always hear me and would never deprive me of Your love. I believe You always answer prayer, though not always in the way I want. Maybe I should be grateful for that. Maybe I don't know what the best outcome is in every situation. Maybe I should let You be God, and I'll be me, doubts and all.

November 11

🦋

Acclaim the Lord, all the earth, serve the Lord gladly, come into
his presence with songs of joy!
Psalm 100:1-2

𝒫salm 100 is one of my favorite psalms. I can picture the Israelites marching around the temple in procession, singing this psalm at the top of their voices. Worship would not be the same without song. When I sing Your praises with the congregation the music adds tremendous force to our words. The combined sound of the organ and our voices singing full out creates a palpable joy that touches me deeply. I hope that You feel it, too, and are glad when we praise You in song.

November 12

Know that he, the Lord, is God, he made us and we
belong to him, we are his people, the flock
that he pastures.
Psalm 100:3

This line of the psalm is so joyful, confident and affectionate, like a little child in the arms of a parent declaring to all, "This is my Mommy!" Is there anyone I could be closer to than You, the One who made me? Parents don't make their children, they conceive them; You make the child. Is there anything You would tend more carefully and lovingly than one whom You have created? Safe as a sheep atop the shoulders of her shepherd, I declare to one and all that I belong to You.

November 13

*Walk through his porticoes giving thanks, enter his courts
praising him, give thanks to him, bless his name!*
Psalm 100: 4

$\mathcal{Y}$esterday, I felt confident, and fearless. Curiously, today's verse from the same psalm elicits the opposite sensation. When I was a toddler, I walked with my mother up the aisle to take a seat toward the front of the church. Not knowing that I was expected to be absolutely silent, I spoke something out loud to her. Retribution was swift. To this day, I cannot walk into a church without feeling constrained, yet this psalm paints a picture of unrestrained joy in worship. The idea is a little alarming, but I'm willing to try. Teach me to enter Your courts with thanks, and without fear.

November 14

*Yes, the Lord is good, his love is everlasting, his
faithfulness endures from age to age.*
Psalm 100:5

*L*ike most people, I long for true love, the love that will
never let me down. When I find love I am ecstatic; then
there is a letdown. The other person cannot read my mind.
She or he does not put my interests above all other interests.
I feel betrayed. The problem is not with them, it's with me,
who wants a human to provide the love of which only You
are capable. Only You can always be good. Only You are
forever faithful. You hold my interests paramount because
those interests are the same as Yours: life to the full in
intimate relationship. Next time I go looking for true love in
the wrong places, help me remember this.

November 15

Bless the Lord, my soul, bless his holy name, all that is in me!
Bless the Lord, my soul, and remember all his kindnesses.
Psalm 103:1-2

*W*hat a beautiful song of praise, written by a heart overflowing with love and gratitude. But how can I bless You, the Source of all life, the Bestower of all blessings? I ask You for things. You need nothing. Right? No? What could You possibly need from me?

> What can I give him, poor as I am?
> If I were a shepherd I would bring a lamb;
> If I were a wise man I would do my part;
> Yet what I can I give him, give my heart. [2]

---

[2]"In the Bleak Midwinter," words by Christina Rossetti, music by Gustav Holst, in *Carols For Christmas*, compiled and arranged by David Willcocks, Metropolitan Museum of Art, (New York, Holt, Rinehart and Winston; 1983).

November 16
Margaret, Queen of Scotland

"The just man shall correct me in mercy and shall reprove me;
but let not the oil," that is, the flattery,
"of the sinner fatten my head." [3]
– Margaret, Queen of Scotland

The reward of humility is the fear of the Lord,
riches, honor and life.
Proverbs 22:4

*H*ow many people, much less sovereigns, would admit being vulnerable to the sin of pride? And how many would express their vulnerability so amusingly? The secret to Margaret's humility might have been her experience as a wife and mother of eight children. Saints without children have to practice humility; mothers live it every day. When motherhood feels overwhelming help me reach out to You.

---

[3] Turgot, Bishop of St. Andrews, *Life of St. Margaret, Queen of Scotland,* William Paterson, Edinburgh, p. 43 (Internet Archive, University of Toronto Library), http://www.archive.org/stream/lifeofstmargaret00turguoft#page/42/mode/2up

November 17

*Not by us, Lord, not by us, by you alone is glory deserved, by
your love and your faithfulness!*
Psalm 115:1

*W*hen I am able to accomplish a difficult, long-anticipated goal, I typically react by saying, "Thank God!" I'm reluctant to acknowledge my contribution to the outcome. Is this humility? A feeling of unworthiness? A superstitious fear that frank acknowledgment of my hard work will result in the goal being snatched away? Of course, without You there would be no good. But, just as You needed Abraham, Moses, and Mary, mother of Jesus, You need me to say "yes" to accomplish Your purposes. When I cooperate with You to bring some good into the world, I feel Your pleasure along with my own. Thanks be to God!

November 18
Hilda, Abbess of Whitby

*"All who knew her called her mother because of her
outstanding devotion and grace."* [4]
— Venerable Bede

*By the grace of God I am what I am, and his grace toward
me has not been in vain.*
1 Corinthians 15:10

*E*xcept on Mother's Day, I rarely hear praise of mothers. Motherhood is an inherently selfless undertaking, a step more irrevocable than marriage, yet the selfless acts of mothers are largely hidden, even from themselves. Bede could see what was hidden. He understood that devotion and grace are the essence of motherhood. Hilda might reply that whatever virtues she exhibited were due to Your grace. By Your grace I am a mother. I thank you for that great blessing and pray that Your grace toward me has not been in vain.

---

[4] http://en.wikipedia.org/wiki/Hilda_of_Whitby

November 19
Elizabeth, Princess of Hungary

"Constant in her devotion to God, Elizabeth's strength was consumed by her charitable labours, and she passed away at the age of twenty-four, a time when life to most human beings is just opening." [5]

You will have the strength, based on his own glorious power, never to give in, but to bear anything joyfully, thanking the Father who has made it possible for you to join the saints and with them inherit the light.
Colossians 1:11-12

Once you start volunteering, it's hard to know when enough is enough. The idea that I might have a life of my own sounds selfish and shallow: what could be more important, more meaningful, than helping the poor and unfortunate? How better could I prove my devotion to You? Sometimes I forget that I don't need to justify my existence; Jesus has done that. Maybe if I stopped running around so much, I could hear Your invitation: "What I want is love, not sacrifice; knowledge of God, not holocausts." (Hos 6:6)

---

[5] *The Catholic Encyclopedia Online*, http://www.newadvent.org/cathen/05389a.htm

November 20

*How I rejoiced when they said to me, "Let us go to the house
of the Lord!" And now our feet are standing in
your gateways, Jerusalem.*
Psalm 122:1-12

Going to church is not a duty or a chore for me, it is a joy, in
spite of my childhood self-consciousness. I need to pray the
liturgy and sing the hymns with others who love You. Before
the mass begins, I sit and give thanks to You for this place
and these people, aware that, whatever our ups and downs
together, my life would be sadly lacking without them. Like
other love relationships, You and I need the support of others
to stay strong together. Jerusalem is here, the time is now.
Let's go.

November 21

🎎

*Mary took a pound of costly perfume made of pure nard,
anointed Jesus' feet, and wiped them with her hair.
John 12:3*

*W*hat a loving, intimate, and frankly sensual way to give thanks. Nard was an ingredient in the incense used for the temple sacrifice. Today it is used in palliative care to help ease the transition from life to death.[6] This Mary was the sister of Lazarus, whom Jesus raised from the dead. Now, in a profound gesture of thanks and love, Mary prepares Jesus for death. What a privilege to touch the feet of Jesus! In the words of the psalmist, how can I make a return to You for all the good You have done for me? (Ps 116:12) Help me to hear Your still, small, voice, and respond.

---

[6]http://en.wikipedia.org/wiki/Spikenard

November 22
St. Cecelia, Martyr

O flute that throbs with the thanksgiving breath
Of convalescents on the shores of death.
O bless the freedom that you never chose.[7]
—W.H. Auden

Blessed be the God of Shadrach, Meshach and Abednego: he has
sent his angel to rescue his servants who, putting their trust in
him, defied the order of the king, and preferred to
forfeit their bodies rather than serve or
worship any god but their own.
Daniel 3:28

*I*t is possible to be grateful for death. This is true even of those who are not martyrs walking joyfully into the fiery furnace. Although it is usually hard for the living to choose it, death means freedom from illness and suffering. St. Paul longed for death to free him from the burden of existence so that he could finally see face to face the One whom he loved and served but never saw in life. (2 Cor 5:4) I don't long for death, but the thought of seeing You face to face fills me with joy. I pray that when death does come, I will have the grace to welcome it as a gift.

---

[7] W.H. Auden, *Three Songs to St. Cecelia* (out of print). See http://en.wikipedia.org/wiki/Hymn_to_St._Cecelia

November 23

🦋

He took the seven loaves and the fish and having given thanks
he broke them and gave them to the disciples, and the disciples
gave them to the crowds, and everyone ate
and they were satisfied.
Matthew 15:36–37

If, as I imagine, the miracle of the manna in the desert
foreshadows Thanksgiving, surely the miracle of the loaves
and fishes does also. Matthew's description is surprisingly
spare for an event so wondrous. Jesus accomplishes this
amazing feat without fanfare, anticipating the eucharist more
formally inaugurated at the Last Supper. The people were
not only fed, they were satisfied, a more soulful state than
being full. When I shop for food, prepare and eat it, help me
remember that recipe for creating a taste of Your kingdom:
food + thanks to You + sharing = satisfaction for all.

November 24

✿

Having taken bread and given thanks he broke it and gave it to
them saying, "This is my body being given for you.
Do this in my memory."
Luke 22:19

*A*nother proto-Thanksgiving; here, a Seder, but with words
that were never heard before, words so new and shocking
that the disciples struggled unsuccessfully to grasp Jesus'
meaning. With the wine, this bread is at the heart of the
Great Thanksgiving, the eucharist, a cosmic thanksgiving
that continues to unfold across time and space, enfolding me
with all creation: this is my body. Words fail. I can only *do*
this in memory of You.

November 25

*Having taken a cup and giving thanks he gave it to them
and they all drank of it and he said, "This is my blood of the
covenant which is being poured out for many."
Mark 14:23-24*

*I*t's so interesting: Jesus is You in the mystery of the Trinity,
yet before He distributes loaves and fishes, or bread and wine,
He thanks You. There is something necessary and powerful
in thanking You. Jesus thanks You for the gift of wine which
becomes His blood, that is also the blood of the covenant
between You and Your people. Up to now the blood of animals
and of circumcised males sealed the covenant. Now, Jesus'
blood alone seals the covenant, even before His crucifixion.
Again, the gift far exceeds the ability of my words to express
gratitude; nevertheless, may I never forget the necessity and
power of thanking You in all I do.

November 26

✣

*I thank you, Lord, with all my heart, because you have
heard what I said.
Psalm 138:1*

Being alone doesn't make me feel lonely; being with other
people and feeling that no one cares what I have to say, as if I
don't exist, that makes me feel lonely. The one who hears and
understands gives life to me. When I know that I have been
heard, I may continue to suffer but I can bear it much better.
It took a long time for me to understand that You always
hear me, although sometimes I have my doubts. In those
moments when I feel You have heard me, my whole being
comes alive with gratitude and joy. Do You ever feel unheard
and unloved? Help me remember to take time each day to
listen to You, and to thank You with all my heart.

November 27

🙦

I do not cease to give thanks for you as
I remember you in my prayers.
Ephesians 1:16

*M*y prayer list is long: family, friends, people in need whom I have heard about, even nations. Occasionally I wonder if it is necessary to pray for each person every day. You know who they are! If I only needed to rely on Your omniscience, I would not need to do anything, ever. As my teacher, the late Sofia Cavalletti, said, You need my conscious cooperation.[8] You gave me the gift of prayer so I can work for the kingdom even when direct action is out of my hands. Prayer helps me to feel more empowered. Prayer reminds me that I am rich in family and friends. May I never cease to give thanks for everyone I remember in prayer.

---

[8] Sofia Cavalletti, *History's Golden Thread; the History of Salvation*, (Chicago, Liturgy Training Publications, 1999), p. 6.

November 28
Emma, Queen of Hawaii

*"Our beloved Church regards her children as having bodies as
well as souls to be cared for."* [9]
–Queen Emma

*Therefore my heart is glad, and my soul rejoices; my
body also rests secure.*
Psalm 16:9

*H*ow refreshing to see the church honor a woman who was
a wife and mother; who was not a martyr nor a woman who
worked herself to death; who understood that the body is
sacred as well as the soul. Moreover, in these days of learning
about holistic health she reminds me that the health of
body is linked not only to the psyche, but also to the soul.
In an over-scheduled life, it is easy to drop the one thing
that seems like it doesn't show. The psalmist says that life
in Your kingdom requires physical, emotional, and spiritual
health. When I am tempted to neglect my body, heart, or
soul, because I am too busy, give me the courage to take care
of myself.

---

[9] George S. Kanahele, *Emma: Hawai'i's Remarkable Queen: A Biography,*
(University of Hawaii Press, 1999), p. 162.

November 29—Dorothy Day

※

"We know Him in the breaking of bread, and we know each other in the breaking of bread, and we are not alone any more. Heaven is a banquet and life is a banquet, too, even with a crust, where there is companionship." [10]
–Dorothy Day

When he was at the table with them, he took bread, blessed and broke it, and gave it to them. Then their eyes were opened, and they recognized him.
Luke 24:30-31(a)

*E*ucharist eases the pain of loneliness. Dorothy Day, who made companionship to the poor her life's work, found companionship and a luxurious feast in eucharist. There, too, is the relief that one is not only invited but belongs, and the intimate joy of Christ's presence: the "Spirit in the bread" and the "fire in the wine." The man who wrote that description, Ephraem the Syrian, a theologian of the early church, also called eucharist "the medicine of life." [11] Sunday can be a lonely day, but I have a standing invitation to dine with You and Your people at Your table where a foretaste of the heavenly banquet awaits.

---

[10] Dorothy Day, *The Long Loneliness, The Autorbiography of the Legendary Catholic Social Activist* (New York; Harper & Row, Publishers, Inc.; 1952), p. 285.

[11] Griffith, Sidney H., "'Spirit in the Bread; Fire in the Wine': the Eucharist as 'Living Medicine' in the Thought of Ephraem the Syrian," Modern Theology 15:2 April 1999.

November 30

✵

Rejoice always, pray without ceasing, give thanks in everything; for this is the will of God in Christ Jesus for you.
1 Thessalonians 5:16-18

Give thanks in everything? Can Paul really mean that? How is it possible to be grateful for illness, poverty, or loss? Is it only saints like Paul who can be genuinely thankful for everything? Paul answers:

> For I am certain of this: neither death nor life,
> no angel, no prince, nothing that exists, nothing
> still to come, not any power, or height or depth,
> nor any created thing, can ever come between
> us and the love of God made visible in Christ
> Jesus our Lord. (Rom 8:38-39)

Can I believe that? I guess don't need to; I will see it for myself. "Then the glory of the Lord shall be revealed, and all people shall see it together."(Is 40:5) Amen. Alleluia.

December :
the Season of Advent —
Preparing for the Light

December 1

A voice cries out: "In the wilderness
prepare the way of the Lord, make straight in the desert
a highway for our God."
Isaiah 40:3

*I*f You are already everywhere, why do I need to prepare a
way for You? Jesus said that in order to enter Your kingdom
we must be born anew. (Jn 3:3) My relationship with You
is not static; over time, my understanding of You has grown
and deepened. The feasts of the church year give me new
opportunities to grow in my relationship with You. Every
Advent, You invite me to prepare the unexplored spaces in
my heart for Christ to be born anew. I pray in joyful hope,
anticipating the spiritual gifts You hide in the hollow of Your
hand, waiting patiently until I am ready to receive them.
What will You give me this Christmas? I can hardly wait!

December 2

Awake, awake! Clothe yourself in strength.
Isaiah 51:9

Like sleeping children, we are told to wake up and get dressed. The letter to the Ephesians warns, "Sleeper, awake! Be very careful about the sort of lives you lead, like intelligent and not like senseless people."(Eph 5:14-15) Regardless of whether I wake or sleep, the light of Christ will be born anew this Christmas. If I want to receive the full benefit of that precious gift, I need to take stock of my life, know what I'm working toward, and make intelligent choices. Like a parent, You are standing next to the bed, waiting for me to wake up, and holding the strength with which You will cloak me. Thank you for caring so much about me.

December 3

The time has come: you must wake up now: our
salvation is even nearer. The night is almost over,
it will be daylight soon.
Romans 13:11-12

When the night is almost over, that's when it seems hardest to wake up. Five more minutes, please! It's hard to imagine that day is coming soon. Paul is standing over my bed, shaking my shoulder, and telling me the good news. He is like that, lecturing me about one thing or another; I, like a teenager, am only half-listening, part of me wishing he'd go away and leave me in peace. Also like a teenager, I know he lectures me because he loves me and wants the best for me, the same as You do. Thank You for sending Paul to help me see the light.

December 4

*Get you up to a high mountain, O Zion, herald of
good tidings; lift up your voice with strength, O Jerusalem,
herald of good tidings, lift it up,
do not fear; say to the cities of Judah, "Here is your God!"*
Isaiah 40:9

Time after time, throughout salvation history, Your people find You on the mountain. Jesus went up the mountain to pray to You. There You helped him repulse Satan's temptation; there He was transfigured and revealed as the Messiah. I am most comfortable with my American, private faith, but Isaiah challenges me to move out of my comfort zone. This news is too wonderful to keep to myself. Where is the high place where I can announce Your presence? In Jesus' final appearance to the disciples, on a mountain, He told them, "Go, make disciples of all the nations, and know that I am with you always."(Mt 28:16-20) The high place is any place I can proclaim Your presence. Give me the courage today to share the good news with someone.

December 5

※

Did you not know, had you not heard? Was it not told you from the beginning?
Isaiah 40:21

"Are you the only one in Jerusalem who doesn't know what's happened?" Luke 24:18

"Oh, how foolish you are, and how slow of heart to believe."
Luke 24:25

*H*iding in plain sight all around me, Your kingdom often escapes my notice. I know that, yet when I need to make judgments and act on them I sometimes forget You. I can't see what You see: the big picture. When, like the disciples on the road to Emmaus, I am tempted to fear and doubt what I already know, walk with me. Remind me that I am not a helpless victim of fate. Christ's birth, death, and resurrection have empowered me to play a unique role in bringing Your kingdom. Renew the flame of my faith, and help me to feel its warmth and light filling my soul.

December 6

❧

See, I am doing a new deed, even now it comes to light;
can you not see it?
Isaiah 43:19

*W*hen a word is repeated in the Bible it is very important. Here, the word, "see" is repeated. There is more than one way to see: there is outer and inner sight, "in-sight." Paul illuminates, praying that Jesus, "may give you a spirit of wisdom and revelation, so that, with the eyes of your heart enlightened, you may know what is the hope to which he has called you, and what is the immeasurable greatness of his power for us who believe."(Eph 1:17-19) Jesus has given me insight to see a new hope within me, founded not on fantasy or whim, but on the greatness of His power. If I close my eyes now I can see that hope, lit by the dawning rays of the light of Christ.

December 7

*See, I am sending my messenger to prepare the way
before me. The messenger of the covenant in whom
you delight—indeed, he is coming, says the Lord of hosts.*
Malachi 3:1

*I*f you are, as my childhood catechism stated, all-powerful, why do You need a messenger? Jesus said that John the Baptist is the messenger prophesied in this scripture; moreover, John is also Elijah, the forerunner of the Messiah. (Lk 7:27) If John was Elijah, that meant Jesus was the Messiah, a shocking idea in Jesus' day. No wonder You sent a messenger to prepare the way. I wonder who Your messengers are today? As Advent progresses, help me to recognize and hear Your messengers, and enable them to prepare the way for Christ to be born anew in my heart this Christmas.

December 8

✿

Then the eyes of the blind shall be opened,
the ears of the deaf unsealed, then the lamb shall leap like a deer
and the tongues of the dumb sing for joy.
Isaiah 35:5-6

*I*magine what it would be like to be blind from birth, never having seen nor understood what the word "see" means; to have known only silence, with no idea what it is to hear; never to be able to speak, only to grunt and groan. What I see is a partial glimpse of the kingdom in which I live; what I hear is a tiny fraction of the spectrum of sound; what I say and sing is a pale shadow of the beauty of which I am capable. The prophet tells me that I live in a kingdom so much greater than I can now perceive. Isaiah creates the desire that engenders the hope that becomes my prayer: come, Lord Jesus! Come quickly!

December 9

*Every valley shall be lifted up, and every mountain
and hill be made low; the uneven ground shall become level,
and the rough places a plain; then the glory of God shall be
revealed and all shall see it.*
Isaiah 40:4-5

What would the world be like if all the highs and lows were leveled? After spending time with a friend who needed a cane, then a walker, and then a wheelchair, I saw how even a small step can become an insurmountable obstacle. There are many of these obstacles, small and large, of one type or another. For a couple of years a condition prevented me from driving by myself for more than half an hour. Some places could be reached by public transportation but it took twice as long. Other places had no public transportation and, without a ride, I couldn't go there. I did what I could and did not complain, but I felt diminished. Your glory, the weight of Your presence, will be revealed when all can see it, not only the able-bodied and sound of mind. Let it be so!

December 10

I will turn the wilderness into a lake, and dry ground
into waterspring.
Isaiah 41:18

*W*hen the Israelites were in exile in Babylon, You promised that, just as You provided water in the desert after the Exodus, you would do so as they returned to the promised land. At Jacob's well, Jesus told the Samaritan woman, "those who drink of the water that I will give them will never be thirsty. The water that I will give will become in them a spring of water gushing up to eternal life."(Jn 4:14) Your ancient promise of the fulfillment of present needs is fulfilled through the presence of Christ within me. Within the well of my heart the life of Christ springs eternally. When I feel lost in the wilderness of Christmas preparations, I need only take a moment to tap the water of life that wells within me, as close as my heart.

December 11

My salvation shall come like the light.
Isaiah 51:5

One has to know dark to appreciate light. It's dark during Advent, when the light is "coming." The sun rises late and sets early. Even the day seems dark. Electric light is cold comfort; a candle more warming with my cup of tea. Isaiah keeps me company in the dark. I can just see the light of his candle ahead of me as I tread the uncertain ground. He has walked this way before me. "Keep going," he seems to say, "don't give up." All the while, You are there, within me, surrounding me, a blazing Light that, for some mysterious reason, needs to be born again and again and again within me until I know You are always there.

December 12
Feast of Our Lady of Guadalupe

*"I am truly your merciful Mother, yours and all the people who
live united in this land and of all the other people of different
ancestries, my lovers, who love me, those who seek me,
those who trust in me."* [1]
– Mary, Our Lady of Guadalupe

*He is like a shepherd feeding his flock, gathering
lambs in his arms, holding them against his breast and leading
to their rest the mother ewes.*
Isaiah 40:1

It is said that every woman needs a wife. So does every
woman need a mother, both human and divine. In times of
deprivation and fear I have taken refuge in the arms of my
Holy Mother, Our Lady of Guadalupe. Her face, so beautiful
yet utterly of-this-earth, gazes at me with deep compassion.
She cares for me with with tenderness, affection, and
untiring attention. How grateful I have been for her love and
protection! I thank You for providing me Your own mother
to turn to when I need the motherly care that no human
mother can give.

---

[1] http://www.theotokos.org.uk/pages/approved/words/wordguad.html

December 13
St. Lucy, Martyr

St. Lucy is one of seven women, aside from the Blessed Virgin Mary, commemorated by name in the Canon of the Mass. Hagiography tells us that Lucy was a Christian martyr during the Diocletian persecution (303 - 313 C.E.). She consecrated her virginity to God through pious works, refused to marry a pagan betrothed, and had her wedding dowry distributed to the poor. [2]

I have appointed you as a covenant of the people and light of the nations, to open the eyes of the blind, to free captives from prison, and those who live in darkness from the dungeon.
Isaiah 42:6

Lucy, patron saint to the blind, reminds me of the power of inner sight. Two blind men sitting by the road cried out to Jesus, "Lord, have mercy on us, Son of David!" Though their blindness was probably obvious, Jesus asked what they wanted Him to do for them. They answered, "Lord, let our eyes be opened." Moved with compassion, Jesus touched their eyes. Immediately, they regained their sight and followed him. (Mt 20:30-34) Unlike many, the two blind men saw who Jesus was. Perhaps His compassion was tinged with gratitude? At any rate, each man received both inner and outer healing. I can see with my eyes, but do I really see who You are? Let my eyes be opened.

---

[2] http://en.wikipedia.org/wiki/St._Lucy

December 14

𝔏

The night is far gone, the day is near. Let us then lay aside
the works of darkness and put on the armor of light.
Romans 13:12

I'm asleep, warm in bed, dreaming. Suddenly, I hear a loud voice, "Wake up! Hurry, the day is near." Startled, I throw off the heavy covers and sit on the side of the bed. Who was that? I gaze around the room, blinking, still half-asleep. Was it a dream? It felt so real. Maybe I should just go back to sleep. I feel for my bathrobe on the bed. There, in the darkness, lies, not my robe, but . . . what? This is strange. A little heap of fabric glows faintly, as if from an inner light. It feels warm, soft, silky -- irresistible. I pick it up, hold it in front of me; it is silvery and lighter than air. Maybe it wasn't a dream. I put it on and feel protected, courageous, and ready to do Your will.

December 15

✣

Those who walk in darkness, and have no light shining for
them, let them trust in the name of the Lord,
let them lean on God.
Isaiah 50:10

When I am walking in darkness it is hard to trust. I can trust when the lights are on and my eyes are wide open. In other words, first prove Yourself to me, then I will decide if I want to trust You; how do I get over that feeling that it is safer not to? I couldn't, if You hadn't reached out to me first. I wouldn't have noticed You reaching out to me if I hadn't been walking in darkness, looking for light. It's a conundrum. Fortunately, I don't need to figure it out. I'm not grateful for the darkness but I'm grateful that, long before I knew I was there and realized I needed someone, You were there with the Light, patiently waiting for me to lean on You.

December 16
O Wisdom, O Sapientia

O Wisdom, which came out of the mouth of the Most High, and reaches from one end to the other, mightily and sweetly ordering all things: Come and teach us the way of prudence. [3]

She is a breath of the power of God, a reflection of the eternal light. Although alone, she can do all; herself unchanging, she makes all things new.
Wisdom 7:25, 27

Today the journey towards Christmas picks up tempo. The O Antiphons, traditional prayers of longing for the Messiah, begin today. [4] Wisdom is a feminine-gendered noun in Latin. In the Book of Wisdom, Solomon relates his search for her: "I prayed, and the spirit of Wisdom came to me." (Wis 7:7) The Hebrew word for spirit is also feminine: *ruach.* "In the beginning, God's spirit hovered over the water. God said, 'Let there be light,' and there was light." (Gen 1:2-3) Just as the ancient generative waters gave birth to light, the generative waters within Mary, over whom Your Spirit hovered, will give birth to the Light. Come to me, sweet Wisdom. Give birth to the Light within me.

---

[3] http://www.umilta.net/sophia.html
[4] http://www.episcopalcafe.com/daily/church_year/sapientiatide_the_great_o_anti.php

December 17— O Adonai

O Adonai and Ruler of the House of Israel, who appeared to Moses in the burning bush and gave him the law in Sinai: come and deliver us with an outstretched arm.

The wolf shall live with the lamb, the leopard shall lie down with the kid, the calf and the lion and the fatling together, and a little child shall lead them.
Isaiah 11:6

*W*ho would have guessed, if Isaiah had not prophesied it, that You would arrive as a little child? I have not seen predator and prey living together yet, but more than one child has led me to greater understanding of Your kingdom. Through years of raising children and contemplating Your word with them, the eyes and ears of my heart were gradually, at times painfully, opened. Jesus said that we will never enter Your kingdom unless we change and become humble like children. (Mt 18:3-4) Living and working with children is humbling and also a door through which I can enter Your kingdom on earth with awe, wonder, and joy. Come, child Jesus, and lead me to Your kingdom.

December 18 — O Root of Jesse

O Root of Jesse, which stands as an ensign of the
people, at whom the kings shall shut their mouths,
and whom the nations shall seek: come deliver us,
do not delay!

*A shoot shall come out from the stump of Jesse, and a branch
shall grow out of his roots.*
Isaiah 11:1

At first glance, a stump means the tree is dead; nevertheless, a shoot grows out of the ancient root stock, David's dynasty. The Hebrew word for stump, *geza*, also refers to the trunk of a living tree. [5] Earlier in Isaiah, this stump is predicted to become a "holy seed." (Is 6:13) Like the grain of wheat in Jesus' parable, something that seems to be dead contains within it life of an entirely new kind, life that, with Jesus' resurrection, will burst forth in a manner almost beyond imagining, without limits of space or time. I am one of the shower of sparks emitted by that explosion, rooted in Christ the Light. O Root of Jesse, deliver me from deadness of spirit to grow in love with You.

---

[5] *The Jewish Study Bible*, p. 807, n.1.

December 19 — O Key of David
— Lillian Trasher, Missionary [6]

O Key of David and Scepter of the house of Israel; bring
out the prisoners and those that sit in darkness
and the shadow of death!

*I will place on his shoulder the key of the house of David; he
shall open, and no one shall shut; he shall shut,
and no one shall open.*
Isaiah 22:22

*I*n the parable of the found sheep, Jesus preaches that, just as
any owner would search for a sheep that is lost, so much more
would the Good Shepherd seek out His lost sheep. (Luke
15:4-10) Jesus made good on this promise when, during his
days in the tomb, he descended into hell to free those held
prisoner there. (1 Pet 3:19) Jesus' death and resurrection were
the keys that freed Him to free those who would otherwise
be forever imprisoned. What did He shut? Maybe the idea
of people being condemned forever. Come, Key of David,
and remind me that no one is beyond Your power to save.

---

[6] http://en.wikipedia.org/wiki/Lillian_Trasher

December 20 — O Day-spring

O Day-spring Brightness of the everlasting Light, Sun
of Righteousness; come to give light to those that sit in
darkness and the shadow of death!

*I will make you the light of the nations so that my salvation
may reach to the ends of the earth.*
Isaiah 49:6

The audacity of this! A tiny embryo hidden within a young
woman hidden within a tiny nation inhabiting barely a speck
on the globe: a spark raised, later raised again to become the
Light of the nations, greater than the light of the sun, dawning
everywhere all at the same time; every spark waiting since
creation to be raised, waiting to be united in one blinding
Light. Let there be light! And there was light, and You saw
it was good, and You named the light, "Jesus, Emmanuel,
God-with-us," and You saw that it was very good and You
said, "This is my Son in Whom I am well pleased." Come,
Day-spring! Come quickly!

December 21 — O King of the Nations

O King and Desire of Nations, O Cornerstone that makes
two one: come to save us whom You have made
of the dust of the earth!

*See how I lay in Zion a stone of witness, a precious
cornerstone, a foundation stone: The believer shall not stumble.
Isaiah 28:16*

*A*braham and Jacob used stones to mark places where
they experienced Your presence. (Gen 12:7, 28:18) Jesus
quoted Psalm 118 when he said, "Have you never read in the
scriptures: 'The stone that the builders rejected has become
the cornerstone; this was the Lord's doing, and it is amazing
in our eyes'?" (Mt 21:42) Christ's death and resurrection
showed Him to be the cornerstone that creates sacred
space beyond time and place. Jesus, a Jew, anchors me, a
Christian, in the foundation of Your people: one flock with
one Shepherd in one sheepfold that is the world. When
I stumble in the search for Your presence, come Desire of
Nations and be my touchstone!

December 22 — O Emmanuel
Charlotte Diggs (Lottie) Moon, Missionary [7]

✠

O Emmanuel, our King and Law-giver: come to save us,
O Lord our God!

They shall name him Emmanuel, which means,
"God is with us."
Matthew 1:23

From Your first steps in the garden in the cool of the day, You sought intimate relationship with Your people. (Gen 3:8) Out of slavery and into freedom You accompanied the Hebrew people, giving them Your constant assurance, "I will be with you." During the exile You continued to assure them through the prophets, "I will be with you." At each step of the journey, Your Presence creates a longing for You to come closer. A crescendo of human desire is met by a sudden shift: Your invitation to unimaginably greater intimacy, foreshadowed in Mary: not only God-with-us, but God within us! O come, Emmanuel, and dwell within me!

---

[7]http://www.bdcconline.net/en/stories/m/moon-charlotte-diggs.php

December 23 — O Virgin of Virgins,
O Daughters of Jerusalem

O Virgin of Virgins, how shall this be? For neither
before you was any like you, nor shall there be after.
Daughters of Jerusalem, why marvel at me?
That which you behold is a
divine mystery.

The Lord himself will give you a sign.
Look, the young woman is with child and shall bear a son.
Isaiah 7:14

The church's fascination with virgins has gotten old, but
this prayer, now out of common use, [8] points to truths that
bear repeating: Jesus was born of an ordinary woman; in His
ministry He was supported financially and accompanied by
ordinary women, even to Calvary; and, upon His resurrection,
first appeared to women who were thus the first to announce
the resurrection. You sent us these signs. The marvel is that
these truths remain in the Bible in spite of centuries of
misogyny; nevertheless, they are seldom noticed, much less
preached upon. O Mother Mary, Daughter of Jerusalem,
inspire me with your courage. Help me to receive the signs,
and say, "Yes."

---

[8] *See* n. 5 above.

December 24 — Christmas Eve

✹

The people that walked in darkness has seen a great light; on
those who live in a land of deep shadow
a light has shone.
Isaiah 9:1

*A*ncient Hebrews believed that all life ended at death;
the dead, called shades, existed somewhere under the earth
in a dark place called Sheol, removed from Your light.[9]
Nevertheless, the psalmist writes, "Though I walk through
the valley of the shadow of death, I fear no harm, for You
are with me." (Ps 23:4)   And in Ps 139, "Where can I flee
from Your presence? . . . if I descend to Sheol, You are there
too." and "darkness is not dark for You; . . . darkness and light
are the same." I hope You are not too disappointed when
I admit that, after all this time, dark is still dark to me and
sometimes I am afraid. Maybe that is why Your Light is so
important to me, such an inexpressibly great gift. There will
be other days on which I think about how I can give back to
You. Tonight I will accept Your gift, enjoy it, and celebrate.

---

[9]*http://en.wikipedia.org/wiki/Sheol#Sheol_in_the_Hebrew_Bible; see, Is. 14:9*

December 25 — Christmas Day

*For there is a child born for us, a son given to us and
dominion is laid on his shoulders.*
Isaiah 9:5-6

*H*ow could the hopes of the world hang on the shoulders of
a child? I never thought much about the reality of this until I
had a baby. Impossible! And yet ... "'Who is the greatest
in the kingdom of heaven?' He set a child in the midst of
them." (Mt 18:1-2) Who is this Child? A human baby and
also Mighty God. What is a baby like? Tiny, frighteningly
vulnerable, but also powerful, in her own way; like You,
capable of great love, and of evoking great love. What are
You trying to tell me? Not that a great man, like King David,
was once a baby, but that the baby Himself is great. How
can I begin to penetrate such a great mystery? It is a gift like
the precious pearl, wrapped in many layers, to be unwrapped
slowly, rapturously, over a lifetime.

December 26

❧

You have made their gladness greater, you have made
their joy increase.
Isaiah 9:2

*W*hat does joy have to do with it? During my childhood, the focus of religion seemed to be entirely on suffering: Jesus', mine, and others'. I thought the point of life was to try not to go to hell. How amazed I was to find that Jesus' own words tell a different story: "I have said these things to you so that my joy may be in you, and that your joy may be complete." (Jn 15:11) It makes sense. How else would Your people know that the prophecies had been fulfilled if Jesus had not made their gladness greater and their joy increase? Thank you for the gift of joy that no one can take away from me. (Jn 16:22)

December 27

For the yoke that was weighing on her, the bar across her
shoulders, the rod of her oppressor, these you
break as on the day of Midian.
Isaiah 9:3

𝓕reedom is another gift of Christmas: freedom from the oppression of others, and -- more insidious -- from my own oppression of myself. I engage in magical thinking, trying to control the outcome of my life by fulfilling the expectations of others. In trying to be "good," expecting love in return, I oppress myself and others. It took me a long time to realize that wasn't love, to realize that the love I longed for could only come from You. When I discovered that Your love had always been mine, I escaped the yoke of expectations and began to move freely in Your kingdom. I discovered the meaning of, "I am the gate. Anyone who enters through me will be safe: he will go freely in and out and be sure of finding pasture." (Jn 10:9)

December 28

This is the name they give him: Wonder Counselor,
Mighty God, . . .
Isaiah 9:6

*W*ho is this child who is born to us? Both less and more than expected. An ordinary child yet King of all creation. A tiny, helpless baby, born in obscurity and also Mighty God. Who is this child? Let me never find myself sure. Let me remain lost in wonder of Him.

December 29

. . . Eternal Father, Prince of Peace.
Isaiah 9:6

There is so much to ponder, so much to enjoy, in the gift of Your Light; so many facets to the diamond, each one dazzling in its splendor. Who is this child? An Eternal Father who rules the peaceable kingdom, "The wolf shall live with the lamb, the leopard shall lie down with the kid, the calf and the lion and fatling together, and a little child shall lead them."(Is. 11:6) Indeed! This kingdom, Your kingdom, is real; the kingdom of this world a passing illusion. For once, Ecclesiastes' vision feels optimistic: yes, all this is vanity and chasing after the wind/ruach/spirit. (Eccles. 1:14) Your Spirit, the spirit of peace, is born again. You reign. On earth as it is in heaven. Amen.

December 30

Wide is his dominion in a peace that has no end, which he establishes and makes secure in justice and integrity.
Isaiah 9:7

*J*ustice and integrity are two more gifts of Christmas. The material inequities portrayed in Dickens' *A Christmas Carol* make visible the grinding, slow death of poverty and oppression. Toys for tots are nice. Day care for tots is what is really needed. Care packages for homeless vets are nice. Homes and jobs for vets are what justice requires. Dickens' story may seem quaint, dressed in Victorian clothes, a reminder of an earlier, less enlightened time, but put it in today's clothes in city, country, or suburbs, and it's as true today as it was then. Sad, because we supposedly know better because of You. With all my heart, I pray that we unwrap Your gifts of justice and integrity and use them today.

December 31

*Then the glory of the Lord shall be revealed, and all
people shall see it together, for the mouth of the
Lord has spoken.*
Isaiah 40:5

Glory conjures an image rather like the Northern Lights,
accompanied by a harmoniously singing choir of angels
"up there." In Hebrew the word "glory" originally means
"weight" or "heaviness" [10] and is translated Presence, as in
You, Yourself. Your Presence shall be revealed on earth as it
is in heaven (Mt 6:10) for You have spoken; Your Word --
the true Light -- is born and dwells among us. (Jn 1:9,14)
You did not stay "up there" on the mountain but, such was
Your longing for intimacy, You came down to us through a
woman heavy with child. You are here. I long for that day
when I, together with all who ever lived and who ever will
live, see You and feel the glorious weight of Your Presence.

---

[10] *http://en.wikipedia.org/wiki/Glory_%28religion%29*

Acknowledgements

As my mentor, the late Tina Lillig said, God prepares his people slowly and over time. This book has many spiritual mothers. My grandmothers, Delores Lynch and Genevieve Haraburd, were devout Roman Catholics who, along with my parents, Mary Lou and Mack, made prayer a part of my daily life. At St. Louise de Marillac High School in Northfield, Illinois, the Daughters of Charity were models of reverent Christianity in the modern world. At Columbia College, Sonia Bloch invited me to share the Jewish shabbat with her family. I will never forget my amazement that prayer could be so enjoyable: a celebration in the home and with food, no less! It was a powerful revelation, the beginning of an interest that has only grown stronger. In the Christian Family Movement at St. Clement's Church in Chicago, experienced parents, especially Nicole and Steve VanderVoort, helped me learn to observe, judge, and act out the gospel, as I tried to balance my life as a young wife and mother with work outside the home.

I remember vividly the fateful day in September, 1988, when, waiting for my daughter in the teacher's lounge at Alcuin Montessori School, I picked up a North American Montessori Teachers Association magazine and flipped to an article entitled, "The Religious Potential of the Child," by Dr. Sofia Cavalletti. Tina Lillig, a former Alcuin parent and Roman Catholic, together with co-leader, Carol Nyberg-Caraviotis, an Episcopalian, had begun the first regional formation course in the Chicago area for the Catechesis of the Good Shepherd. Taking that course changed my life forever.

The Catechesis is called formation, not education, because we acknowledge the truth of Augustine's words that, in relation to God there is only one Inner Teacher. The catechist, like a matchmaker, creates the environment in which the child and Christ can get to know each other intimately. In the process, the catechist herself may fall in love with God.

So began my love affair with God, with all the ups and downs, joys and disillusionments, that occur in any love affair, with one important difference: God never breaks up. I may forget God, but God will never forget me: "Which one of you, having a hundred sheep and losing one of them, does not leave the ninety-nine in the wilderness and go after the one that is lost until he finds it?" (Lk 15:4) This book is the product of that relationship. Like a love-struck teenager, I have filled dozens, maybe hundreds, of journals with complaints, musings, fears, and attempts at understanding. I have never felt that God doesn't exist. In spite of some terrible tragedies and disappointments, I believe with Paul Wadell that God desires our friendship love, and I have lived into that reality.

In the Catechesis, as in the rabbinic tradition, one's teachers, or formation leaders as we call them, are very important. My formation leaders have been spiritual mothers to me, transmitting the Good Shepherd's call with diligence and devotion. Besides Tina and Carol, they include Carol Dittburner; the late Maria Cristlieb of Mexico; Maria Ludlow, also of Mexico; Rebekah Rojcewicz; Linda Kaeil; and Barbara Searle. In Rome, I was privileged to study with Dr. Sofia Cavalletti, Gianna Gobbi, Tilda Cocchini, Francesca Cocchini, Sylvana Montanaro, and Claudia Margarita Schmitt.

Dr. Sofia Cavalletti, a Roman Catholic, was an eminent Hebrew scholar when a friend asked her to teach her son about the Bible. Cavalletti was a student of the chief rabbi of Rome, Eugenio Zolli, and the first woman to serve on a Vatican commission for Catholic and Jewish relations. She died one year ago, and I can only guess at the degree to which her knowledge of Torah and ancient languages informed her work with the children in the Catechesis. Thanks to my own Torah teacher, Tamar Pelleg, and author and midrashist, Dr. Avivah Gottlieb Zornberg, both of Jerusalem, I am discovering for myself the Jewish tradition of scripture study called midrash. They have opened for me, as a treasure chest, its endless riches: vast and deep, logical and creative, serious and playful, reverent and irreverent, constantly new and surprising, revealing astonishing glimpses of God and self. They have enabled me to take the tools I learned in the Catechesis to a new and delightful level.

God wants us to live in community. In the list of spiritual mothers I must include my sister catechists of the Good Shepherd. Among them, in no particular order, are Barbara Fleming, Pam Moore, Monica Halloran, Carol Bularzik, Catherine Gallogly, Mary Pat Baubly, Pat Heiman, Peggy Plastina, Janice Roberts, Bernadette Freeman (whose work is on the cover of this book), Mary Susan Chen, Margaret Brennan, Kathleen O'Hara, Ave Zuccarino Crow, Margaret Burk, Suzanne Lewis, Diane Hall, Sarah Bond, Polly Tangora, Betsy Peterson, Julianne McCauley, Carol Cade, Joan Roberts, Sarah Hunt, Sara Muriello, and Susan Montgomery.

My publishers Sue and Charles Wells are surely the godparents of this book, having encouraged me and kept me on the right path throughout this year of work. Hollis Bernstein prayed with the drafts and graciously offered comments that improved it. Margaret McCamant's editing expertise refined the finished manuscript.

It is said that our children are our greatest spiritual teachers. Without mine, I would never have found this joyful path. I thank Allison and Ivan Anich, and Sara, Jay, Mason, and Rachel Strom, for their patience, forgiveness, and love.

Finally, I owe this work to the support and vision of my husband, David G. Strom, who, years ago, didn't blink when I told him I was a theology student and asked me out to lunch anyway. Along with many others, I benefit from his loving care and generosity. This book would not exist without him.

Suzanne Haraburd
River Forest, Illinois, 2012

Index of Bible Citations

1 Samuel
1:26-28 — July 26
2:1 — November 4
6:13 — October 24
16:7 — February 11, April 23,
    June 20, July 4
16:13 — May 5

1 Kings
4:29 — March 8

1 Chronicles
16:34 — November 5
17:16 — November 6
29:10 — April 3

2 Chronicles
1:5-12 — May 22

Ezra
3:11-13 — November 2

Job
4:8 — October 9
28:3 — February 25
28:11 — February 25
31:26-27 — September 21
33:4 — May 6

Psalms
5 — July 21
9 — July 11, November 7
16 — January 29, July 8,
    November 28
23 — January 8, February 4,
    November 8, December 24
26 — July 12
27 — March 6
31 — July 15
37 — July 14
41 — July 18

43 — January 3, November 9
45 — May 5, August 15
55 — July 23
56 — July 27, 28
57 — July 30, 31
62 — July 1, 2, 3, 4, 5, 6
63 — June 12, October 15
66 — November 10
73 — April 27, July 16
85 — June 9
91 — August 5
92 — June 2
100 — November 11, 12, 13, 14
103 — November 15
104 — August 12
115 — November 17
116 — November 21
118 — December 21
119 — April 4 , July 7, 10, 13
122 — November 20
126 — October 16
131 — April 25
137 — June 16
138 — November 26
139 — January 11,
    February 1-10, 12-25, 27, 29,
    August 23, December 24
143 — May 12

Proverbs
3:3 - July 9
3:5-6 — January 18
3:17 — March 9
6:22 — February 4
8:1 — January 2
8:2, 4 — March 1
8:6 — March 2
8:11 — March 8
8:12, 14 — March 5
8:17 — January 11, March 6
8:20 — March 7

8:22, 27 — March 3
8:30-31 — March 4
8:32-34 — March 9
8:35 — March 10
9:1 — March 29
9:2 — March 30
9:3, 5 — March 31
10:19 — August 11
16:24 — September 28
22:4 — November 16
22:8 — October 11
22:9 — April 5

Ecclesiastes
1:14 — October 20, December 29
3:1 — September 1
3:2 — September 2, 4
3:3 — September 5, 6
3:4 — September 7, 8
3:5 — September 10, 11
3:6 — September 12, 13
3:7 — September 14, 15
3:8 — September 16, 18

Song of Solomon
2:12 — October 16
4:12 — June 11
4:15 — June 12
4:16 — June 13, 14
5:1 — June 15
6:10 — June 17

Isaiah
6:13 — December 18
7:14 — December 23
9:1-2 — October 14, October 24, December 24, 26
9:3 — December 27
9:5-6 — December 25, 28, 29
9:7 — December 30

11:1-2 — May 17, 18, 19, 20, 21, 22, 23, December 18
11:6 — December 17, 29
11:8 — March 4
11:9 — June 14
12:3 — May 4
14:12 — January 7
22:22 — December 19
25:6 — March 30, October 31
28:16 — December 21
29:18 — May 28
30:15, 18 — April 25
35:5-6 — December 8
40 — May 21
40:1 — December 12
40:3 — December 1
40:3-11 — May 12
40:4-5 — December 9
40:5 — November 30, December 31
40:9 — December 4
40:21 — December 5
41:18 — December 10
42:1 — May 7
42:6 — December 13
42:16 — January 16
43:19 — December 6
44:2 — July 17
44:3 — May 4
44:4 — June 9
45:3 — February 18
45:8 — June 9
48:6 — May 28
49:1, 15 — June 27
49:6 — December 20
50:7-8 — May 30
50:10 — December 15
51:3 — June 7
51:5 — December 11
51:9 — December 2
52:7 — May 25
55:1-3 — April 13, June 24

55:8 — February 20
55:10-11 — March 31
58:8 — June 9
58:9 — April 20
58:10-11 — June 8
60:1 — January 5
61:1, 3 — April 10, May 13
61:11 — June 9

Jeremiah
6:16 — January 23
8:20, 22 — October 13
17:7 — April 6
31:3 — November 4
31:12 — June 10

Ezekiel
2:1-3 — May 30
11:19-20 — May 3
34:11-12 — May 12
36:26 — March 2
36:35 — June 16
37:4-10 — April 26, May 16
47:1 — June 4
47:12 — June 18

Daniel
2:20 — April 7
2:20-21 - September 29
3:24 — November 1
3:28 — November 22
12:3 — January 24

Hosea
6:1-3 — September 14
6:6 — November 19
10:12 — October 12
14:5-7 — June 17

Joel
2:28-29 — May 2

Amos
5:15 — September 16
5:24 — June 8

Jonah
1-2 — February 12

Micah
6:8 — February 2, March 23

Haggai
2:4-5 — May 10

Zechariah
12:10 — May 9

Malachi
3:1 — December 7
3:2 — May 1

Wisdom
6:14-15 — March 13
6:16-17 — March 25
7:7 — March 27, December 16
7:8-9 — March 8
7:14 — March 11, 12
7:22 — March 12
7:23 — March 13
7:24 — March 14
7:25(a) — March 15
7:25, 27 — December 16
7:26 — March 16
7:27 — March 17, 18
7:29 — March 19
8:1 — March 20
8:2, 16 — March 8
8:3 — March 21
8:4 — March 22
9:9(b) — March 23
9:10 — March 24
9:11 — March 26

Mark

1:12 — May 26
3:32-25 — January 15
4:11 — May 14
4:26-28 — June 24 , August 4
4:26-29 — October 2
5:36 — April 6
8:1-9 — April 13
8:18 — May 28
8:35 — September 9
9:7 — January 17, March 1
9:23-24 — March 24
10:31 — August 19
14:23-24 — June 21, November 25
15:34 — October 13
16:15 — September 15

Luke

1:41 — May 31
1:42 — February 16
1:45 — April 19, 29
1:46 — May 27
1:47 — October 15
1:67-78 — May 31
3:21-22 — May 25
4:13-21 — March 10
6:19 — April 11
6:20 — April 9, August 20
6:21(a) — April 14
6:21(b) — April 11
6:25 — April 11
6:35 — February 22
6:36-37 — October 11
6:38 — April 11
7:22-23 — August 21
7:27 — December 7
8:11 — October 22
9:2 — August 22
9:47 — February 20
9:58 — February 26
9:62 — August 26

10:38 — February 26
11:7 — June 11
11:9-10 — August 16
11:28 — April 17
12:22 — August 14
12:27 — June 19
12:31 — August 14
12:37 — April 20
13:18-19 — April 9, June 20,
    August 1
13:29 — August 28
14:27 — March 7
15 — September 8
15:4-10 — May 2, December 19
15:7 — April 19, August 24
15:9 — April 19
15:20 — February 3
15:20-23 — April 23
15:22-24 — April 19
15:32 — June 30
17:20-21 — April 9, August 2
18:1, 7-8 — October 10
18:17 — April 9
18:25 — April 9
22:19 — April 29, November 24
22:42-44 — June 22
23:34 — May 9
24:18 — December 5
24:25 — December 5
24:30-31(a) — November 29

John

1:4-5 — January 25, March 19
1:9, 14 — March 24, 31, April 7,
    December 31
2:21 — September 6
3:3 — August 27, December 1
3:8 — May 24
4:10 — June 4
4:14 — May 4, December 10
4:35-36 — October 17

7:9 — September 11
13:2 — February 7
13:12 — August 23
15:10 — November 18
15:20 — October 27
15:42 — June 29
15:43, 45 — June 28

2 Corinthians
3:18 — March 16
5:4 — November 22
5:17 — March 17, April 2, May 24
9:6 — October 23
9:10 — October 22

Galatians
3:8-9 — April 24
3:28 — June 2
6:9 — October 20

Ephesians
1:9-10 — March 22, April 12,
September 29, October 30
1:16 — November 27
1:17-19 — December 6
1:18 — February 24
4:18 — May 19
5:14-15 — December 2

Philippians
2:5-10 — April 12
2:10 — February 10
4:6-7 — May 19

Colossians
1:11-12 — November 19
1:17-19 — September 30

1 Thessalonians
5:16-18 — November 30

2 Timothy
1:13-14 — May 22

Hebrews
3:7 — March 2
10:22 — February 11

James
2:5 — April 9
3:8-9 — May 18
3:18 — May 18, October 21

1 Peter
1:3 — April 16
1:21 — April 6
3:18 — February 10
3:19 — December 19

2 Peter
1:19 — January 20

1 John
4:18 — May 10, July 24

Revelation
1:3 — April 26
2:26, 28-29 — January 21
14:15 — October 1
21:2-3 — June 17
21:5 — January 14
21:9-10 — June 12
22:16 — January 20, 31
22:17 — March 29, June 11

15457504R00213

Made in the USA
Charleston, SC
04 November 2012